THE FORMER SOVIET UNION:
THEN AND NOW

Ukraine:
Then and Now

Gail B. Stewart

ReferencePoint
Press®

About the Author

Gail Stewart is an award-winning author of more than 250 books for children, teens, and young adults. She lives in Minneapolis, MN, and is the mother of three grown sons.

© 2015 ReferencePoint Press, Inc.
Printed in the United States

For more information, contact:
ReferencePoint Press, Inc.
PO Box 27779
San Diego, CA 92198
www.ReferencePointPress.com

Picture Credits
Cover: Steve Zmina; Akg-images/Newscom: 24; © Ivan Chernichkin/Reuters/Corbis: 60; © Sergey Dolzhenko/epa/Corbis: 40, 57; © Gleb Garanich/Reuters/Corbis: 45; © Heritage Images/Corbis: 17; © Hulton-Deutsch Collection/Corbis: 37; © Sergii Kharchenko/Demotix/Corbis: 63; © Maysun/Corbis: 96; Thinkstock Images: 4, 5; © Reuters/Corbis: 29; © Fyodor Savintsev/ITAR-TASS/Corbis: 32; © Scheufler Collection/Corbis: 52; © Prokofyev Vyacheslav/ITAR-TASS Photo/Corbis: 8; Steve Zmina: 19; Cossacks charging into battle, Roubaud, Franz (1856–1928)/Private Collection/Photo © Christie's Images/Bridgeman Images: 12; *Portrait of the Ukranian Author Taras Grigorievich Shevchenko* (1814-61), 1871 (oil on canvas), Kramskoy, Ivan Nikolaevich (1837–87)/Tretyakov Gallery, Moscow, Russia/Bridgeman Images: 49

LIBRARY OF CONGRESS CATALOGING-IN-PUBLICATION DATA

Stewart, Gail B. (Gail Barbara), 1949–
  Ukraine : then and now / by Gail B. Stewart.
    pages cm. — (The former Soviet Union: then and now series)
  Includes bibliographical references and index.
  ISBN-13: 978-1-60152-708-0 (hardback)
  ISBN-10: 1-60152-708-X (hardback)
  1. Ukraine—Juvenile literature. I. Title.
  DK508.515.S74 2015
  947.7—dc23
                                        2014007770

CONTENTS

1924
Lenin dies; Stalin becomes leader of the Soviet Union.

1922
The Union of Soviet Socialist Republics is created; Soviet troops march into Kiev, claiming Ukraine as one of the first four Soviet Republics.

1928
Stalin announces plan to collectivize farms in Ukraine.

1920	1925	1930	1935	1940

1923
Lenin begins *korenizatsiya*, a program to promote Ukrainian culture.

1932
Stalin begins punishing farmers by orchestrating a famine, killing between 6 and 8 million people.

1926
Stalin bans all religious worship in Ukraine and other Soviet republics.

1941
In June Hitler's army invades Ukraine; September 29–30, Nazi troops exterminate more than thirty-three thousand Jews at Babi Yar.

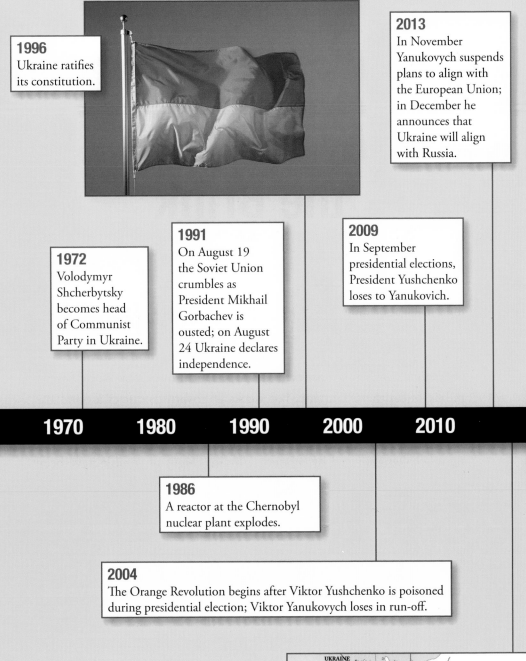

1996
Ukraine ratifies its constitution.

2013
In November Yanukovych suspends plans to align with the European Union; in December he announces that Ukraine will align with Russia.

1991
On August 19 the Soviet Union crumbles as President Mikhail Gorbachev is ousted; on August 24 Ukraine declares independence.

2009
In September presidential elections, President Yushchenko loses to Yanukovich.

1972
Volodymyr Shcherbytsky becomes head of Communist Party in Ukraine.

1970   **1980**   **1990**   **2000**   **2010**

1986
A reactor at the Chernobyl nuclear plant explodes.

2004
The Orange Revolution begins after Viktor Yushchenko is poisoned during presidential election; Viktor Yanukovych loses in run-off.

2014
Russia annexes the Crimean Peninsula; the European Union and the United States condemn the action. Violence between pro-Russian and pro-Ukraine adherents spreads across eastern and southern Ukraine.

5

A Nation on the Brink

Ukraine is a nation on the brink of momentous change. After several tense weeks of protests and violence in Ukraine's capital of Kiev (sometimes spelled Kyiv), Russia, Ukraine's giant neighbor to the east, inserted itself into the controversy in 2014. Defying international warnings and condemnation, Russia annexed Crimea, the autonomous Black Sea republic of southern Ukraine. For weeks afterward countries around the world sought ways to punish Russia and support Ukraine. More than anything else, however, this event illustrates the deep divisions and extreme challenges faced by modern Ukraine. Signs of trouble have been building for a while. In November 2013 the *Maidan*, the large public square in Kiev, was the site of a protest movement. Many Ukrainians were furious about the economic and political actions of their government. At times the crowds in the *Maidan* numbered in the hundreds of thousands as some protesters lobbed rocks at police and set stacks of tires ablaze. Television viewers around the world watched as the violence increased between police and demonstrators.

The following month, on December 26, hundreds of journalists and activists stood outside the Ministry of the Interior's government offices. Many held candles, while others clutched grisly photographs of thirty-four-year-old Tetyana Chornovil, a respected Ukrainian journalist. As they stood in the cold, the protesters demonstrated their outrage at the violent act of the day before—a vicious physical attack on Chornovil. "Shame! Shame!"[1] they yelled, aiming their angry words at the people inside the building.

A Silent Attack

Anyone who knew Chornovil would have had trouble recognizing her from those photographs. Her face was bloodied and battered, one eye blackened, her nose broken, and her lips split and swollen. After beating her, Chornovil's assailants threw her into a ditch and left her there at the side of the road with a concussion and multiple fractures to her nose and face.

According to police, Chornovil had been driving home early in the morning of December 25 when suddenly a car veered in front of her. It blocked her path and then forced her car to the side of the road. As soon as she stopped, several men got out of their car and broke the back window of her car. Her assailants pulled her out of the car and began to beat her.

Chornovil told police she was attacked by at least two men, neither of whom uttered a single word during the beating. "I started running, they began pursuing me," she said in video comments posted on Ukraine's *Pravda* news website. "They were hitting me on the head, they were not saying anything, they were just hitting."[2]

"They were hitting me on the head, they were not saying anything, they were just hitting."[2]

—Journalist and activist Tetyana Chornovil after being beaten.

A Worrisome Trend

Many Ukrainians are certain that the assault on Chornovil was not a random act of violence but rather the latest in a series of attacks against Ukraine's activists and journalists. In 2013 there were reports of more than one hundred acts of violence in Ukraine against journalists who had written blogs or articles finding fault with the government.

Journalists point out that Chornovil had recently written several articles critical of Victor Yanukovych, Ukraine's president at the time. She had also questioned the sudden and unexplained wealth and lavish lifestyles of some of Yanukovych's government ministers. In fact, the day she was attacked she had been working on a story revealing an expensive country manor being built for Ukraine's interior minister, Vitaliy Zakharchenko.

Kiev's Independence Square (or Maidan*) was the site of mass antigovernment protests in February 2014 (pictured). Government forces fired on demonstrators, escalating the crisis in Ukraine—a crisis that gave Russia an opening to annex Crimea.*

Chornovil had sneaked onto the new property and taken photographs that she intended to publish on her website. She and other journalists believe the beating was an effort to prevent her from publishing the story and photographs.

Russia's takeover of Crimea and the physical violence against the media are examples of the tensions—both internal and external—that are threatening to tear Ukraine apart. For decades this nation of 46 million people has been dealing with massive corruption by its political leaders. The country is also deeply divided about its future direction. About two-thirds of the population are ethnic Ukrainians; nearly one-third are ethnic Russians; the remainder includes other groups such as Poles, Greeks, Bulgarians, and Jews. All of these populations have different ideas about how Ukraine should be governed and by whom. The future of Ukraine, which had once seemed very bright, is now cloaked in uncertainty.

In a press conference on April 17, 2014, US secretary of state John Kerry noted the challenges Ukraine is facing, declaring, "The Ukrainian people now deserve a right to choose their own future."[3] Ukraine in the twenty-first century is struggling with a range of difficult problems. Some are the ghosts of tragedies that occurred when Ukraine was part of the Soviet Union, while others—economic issues and widespread corruption, for instance—have more recent beginnings. It is the hope of many Ukraine citizens that they will have the strength to change the direction their nation is going.

CHAPTER ONE

The Most Coveted Land

The modern nation of Ukraine is fairly new; it was in 1991 that Ukraine declared its independence from the Soviet Union. However, the land that is now Ukraine has a very long, violent, and difficult history. It has been dominated by other nations and has been influenced by many cultures—almost always against the will of the Ukrainian people.

A Land of Plenty to a Mighty Kingdom

From earliest times, tribes of nomadic people began to move into the region that is Ukraine. They were drawn to the rich, fertile soil; the deep forests; and the bounty of the land. Notes journalist Anna Reid: "Leave a plough in a field overnight, it was said, and the next morning you couldn't find it again for new grass. So numerous were the bison that hunters didn't even bother to eat the meat, just taking the hides. So packed were the rivers with fish that a spear would stand upright, unsupported, in the water."[4]

Slavic people were likely the first to settle in Ukraine, but it was a Viking prince named Kyi and his two siblings who founded the city of Kiev in the seventh century CE. They turned it into a bustling and prosperous trade center. Using their longboats, the Rus (Slavs referred to Vikings by the word "rus" meaning "to row") moved goods down the Dnipro River to the Black Sea. That became an important trade route from Northern Europe south to the Byzantine Empire. The kingdom that developed around the busy center of Kiev became known as Kyivan Rus. Kiev remains Ukraine's capital today.

Fighting Outside Domination

But the natural resources that had made Ukraine so attractive to Slavic people who settled and farmed there continued to draw outsiders determined to take the land for themselves. Beginning in the fourteenth century, Lithuania and Poland both sought to dominate sections of Ukraine. By the late sixteenth century the two countries had merged into the Polish-Lithuanian Commonwealth. Through that union Poland was able to gain control of all of Lithuania's Ukraine holdings in the western part of the country.

Life changed dramatically for the people of Ukraine under Polish rule. Once farmers who toiled on their own plots of land, Ukrainians were suddenly relegated to the status of serfs, working without pay on large Polish-owned farms. There were cultural changes, too. The native Ukrainian language was replaced by Polish, and the Orthodox religion was supplanted by Catholicism.

> "Leave a plough in a field overnight, it was said, and the next morning you couldn't find it again for new grass."[4]
>
> —Journalist and historian Anna Reid.

Over the years Ukrainians chafed under the harsh treatment of their masters. Beginning in the fifteenth century some of the serfs escaped from Polish-controlled western Ukraine. They fled to the southeastern part of the steppe, a largely uninhabited area. There they formed highly skilled guerilla-style fighting groups. With their fierce battle techniques—most of which were accomplished on galloping horses—they became successful warriors. They called themselves *kazaks* (Turkish for "free men" or "adventurers"), or Cossacks. As their fighting bands increased throughout the Ukraine steppe, the Cossacks would have a very important role in Ukraine over the next 350 years.

The Cossacks

Runaway serfs were not the only ones to join the Cossacks. A variety of misfits and escaped convicts gravitated to the steppe to be part of the group. Reid says that in many ways, with their amazing skills at fighting on horseback, the Cossacks became as important to Ukrainian legend as cowboys are to American legend. "They ranged the steppe in covered wagons, drawing them up in squares in case of . . . attack," she writes. "They wore splendid moustaches, red boots and baggy trousers 'as wide as the Black Sea.' They danced, sang, and drank *horika* [vodka] in heroic quantities."[5]

Cossacks elected their own leaders, known as *hetmans*, and discussed their military plans and strategies around their campfires. They did not pledge eternal alliance with any particular country or political party. Instead, they voted on whether an issue was worth fighting for. During the seventeenth century Cossacks made frequent attacks on the Polish army in Ukraine, yet they occasionally fought on behalf of Poland when the Turks or other armies invaded Polish territory.

Though the Cossacks were often successful, they did suffer occasional losses. For example, the Polish government was furious at the Cossacks' constant attacks on landholders in Ukraine, and it occasionally mounted bloody retaliatory strikes against them. "The Cossacks are the fingernails of our body politic," a Polish noble once explained. "They tend to grow too long and need frequent clipping."[6]

Cossacks on horseback charge into battle. Ukraine's Cossacks sought military support from the Russian czar in exchange for a pledge of allegiance to Russia.

Bohdan Khmelnytsky's Mistake

In the mid-seventeenth century the most famous Cossack leader, Bohdan Khmelnytsky, led his warriors in carving out their own territory within the Polish-controlled area of Ukraine. Khmelnytsky knew that the Cossacks would have difficulty holding the territory for long without outside help. That is when he made a tactical error in judgment that would cause Ukraine monstrous problems for centuries to come.

Khmelnytsky asked the Russian czar, Alexander I, for military aid against the Poles. Alexander consented, as long as the Cossack leader would pledge his allegiance to Russia. Khmelnytsky agreed, and in January 1654 he swore an oath that was known as the Agreement of Pereyaslav (the name of the city where the ceremony took place).

> "The Cossacks are the fingernails of our body politic. They tend to grow too long and need frequent clipping."[6]
>
> —Polish noble on his country's ambiguous relationship with the Cossacks.

The czar had no intention of letting Ukraine slip away to the Cossacks. As promised, Russia sent its armies to Ukraine; however, the czar appointed his own governor to rule the region and then joined forces with the Poles. The combined Russian and Polish military easily overcame Cossack resistance. The Russians claimed all Ukraine territory east of the Dnipro River, while the Poles took possession of Ukrainian land west of the river.

By the middle of the eighteenth century internal political turmoil had made Poland weak and vulnerable to outside attacks. Catherine II, now the Russian ruler, saw an opportunity; she sent Russian troops west of the Dnipro River to claim Poland's share of Ukraine. Although Austria also claimed a few small areas of western Ukraine, by 1795 the lion's share of Ukrainian territory had been swallowed up by the mighty Russian Empire.

Difficult Times for "Little Russians"

Catherine immediately began referring to Ukraine as "Little Russia" and its people as "Little Russians." She might have intended it as a way of establishing a bond with Ukraine, but to the people of Ukraine the term was insulting and condescending. She insisted that Ukraine had always been part of Russia, going back eight centuries to the days of Kyivan Rus.

Her goal was to make certain that the people of Ukraine had loyalty only to Russia. One way of ensuring that loyalty was to destroy any shred of devotion they had to the idea of Ukraine as their homeland. The sooner Ukrainian people thought of themselves as Russians, she believed, the sooner they would be grateful to play a key role in the success of the Russian Empire.

Catherine used a variety of approaches to ensure loyalty from the Ukraine people. She offered special privileges to Cossack leaders, allowing them to keep land they had occupied within the former Ukraine territory. She also granted them tax-exempt status for their loyalty and even bestowed titles on them—in effect giving them the status of nobility.

Russification

On the other hand, Catherine and the czars who followed her could be cruelly punitive as well. They made laws designed to wipe out any vestiges of Ukrainian culture. If Ukrainians were to become true "Little Russians," Catherine believed, they must be forced to adopt Russian ways—a process that historians call "Russification." For example, she prohibited Ukrainian Christians from practicing any religion other than Orthodox. Many Ukrainians who had grown up in Polish-controlled western Ukraine had become Catholics, but Catholic churches were banned in Russia.

The most difficult loss concerned language. Catherine issued decrees prohibiting Ukrainian from being taught or spoken in schools, but Czar Alexander II, her immediate successor, went even further. In 1867 he issued the Edict of Ems, which formally banned any public performances such as plays, lectures, and concerts in which the Ukrainian language was spoken or sung. Centuries-old folk songs, very dear to the Ukrainian people, were also banned. Newspapers, magazines, and books written in Ukrainian were removed from shops and libraries and destroyed.

Those Ukrainians who chose not to give up their religion, language, or other customs quickly learned how harsh Catherine and her succes-

Crimea Becomes Russian

The peninsula known as Crimea is the southernmost part of Ukraine, on the northern coast of the Black Sea. Besides its physical distance, there are a number of other ways in which it is remote from the rest of Ukraine. Unlike the Slavic people who dominated Russia and Ukraine, Crimea's early settlers were the descendants of Turkish-speaking warriors, known as Tatars. They arrived with Mongolian Tatars—warriors in the thirteenth century who invaded after the breakup of Kyivan Rus and settled on the Crimean peninsula. The Tatars were ruled by an Islamic political group that answered to the sultan of the Ottoman Empire in Turkey.

However, in the eighteenth century, Russia—with help from the Cossacks—began gobbling up more territory in Crimea. By 1783 Catherine II announced that Crimea had been officially added to the Russian Empire. Soon afterward, Russia began setting up military outposts and bases in Crimea, a strategic boon for Russia because it could control access to the Black Sea. In fact, the domination of the Turks and Tatars in Crimea—Ukraine's southern border—opened the door for Russia's early twentieth-century conquest of Ukraine.

sors could be. Many thousands who dared to voice complaints against Russification were arrested and sent into exile to work as slave laborers in frigid Siberia—never to be heard from again.

World War I

When the First World War broke out in Europe in September 1914, Ukraine was the scene of a great deal of bloodshed. Ukrainians fought in both armies. In western Ukraine 250,000 inhabitants were conscripted into the Austrian army to fight on the side of the Central Powers, led by Germany and Austria. By far the most Ukrainians—3.5 million—were incorporated into the Russian army to fight on the side of the Allies, made up of Russia, France, Great Britain, and later, the United States.

Not only were tens of thousands of Ukrainian soldiers killed in the fighting, some of the bloodiest battles of the war occurred on Ukrainian soil. In the process, millions of civilians were killed or displaced and those who survived were often suspected of treasonous acts during the war. "Accused of collaboration by both sides," notes Reid, "Ukrainian civilians suffered terribly throughout, being shot, deported or interned in thousands."[7]

Russia in Turmoil

As Ukrainians were fighting and dying on both sides during the war, Russia's government was coming apart at the seams. The people of Ukraine, as well as those in other territories under Russian control, seethed at their ravaged economies, mass poverty, and widespread food shortages. They blamed Czar Nicholas II, a weak leader who did as his advisers urged when he took a hard line rather than offering reforms that might have alleviated some of the problems.

Out of this chaotic environment emerged a group known as Bolsheviks, revolutionaries who would be later known as Communists. Led by Vladimir Lenin, the Bolsheviks demanded an end to the government of Czar Nicholas II in early 1917. Lenin promised the Russian people—as well as Ukrainians and others under Russian control—that under communism wealth and prosperity would be shared among all workers. There would be no czar who would live in luxury while people starved. The Bolsheviks' message resonated with millions—from people living in cities and towns without sufficient food to workers demanding economic reforms.

By March 1917 even Russian troops had joined the angry mobs demanding change. Realizing he had no hope of keeping the throne, Czar Nicholas II fled the palace in Petrograd (now called Saint Petersburg). A provisional government was hastily put into place, but Lenin and the Bolsheviks had gained control by October 1917. The reign of the czars was over.

The Right Moment for Independence

Two days after the news of Nicholas's abdicating the throne reached Kiev, a group of Ukrainian leaders began working to gain indepen-

Vladimir Lenin gives a rousing speech during the October 1917 meeting that brought the Bolsheviks to power in Russia. Lenin promised Russians, Ukrainians, and others that they would all share in the prosperity of the new regime.

dence for Ukraine. These leaders created the Central *Rada*, or Council. Members of the Rada had many different ideas about the kind of government that should lead Ukraine. Some wanted a complete break with Russia. Others, especially in the Ukrainian Socialist Revolutionary Party (USRP), wanted to see farmers (or peasants) gain land for farming rather than have the land controlled by wealthy landowners. A more moderate party, the Ukrainian Party of Socialists-Federalists, still wanted to be part of the Russian state but with the ability to make their own decisions.

The provisional government that had taken over after the czar's departure objected, reminding the Rada that it was not an elected body and therefore could not claim to speak for the people of Ukraine. However, members of the Rada bravely announced their intentions in a written decree: "Let Ukraine be free. Without separating themselves entirely from Russia, without severing connections with the Russian state, let the

Ukraine people in their own land have the right to order their own lives. . . . From this day forth we shall direct our own lives."[8]

The Rada's most important job was to choose the Ukrainian president. Their decision was made on April 29, 1918, when they elected historian, author, and scholar Mykhailo Hrushevsky. For years Hrushevsky had championed the right of eastern and western Ukraine to be united as an independent nation. Jubilant at the idea of independence and excited by their new president, hundreds of thousands of Ukrainians poured into the streets celebrating and waving blue and yellow flags, the new symbol of the Ukraine National Republic.

"Let Ukraine be free. . . . From this day forth we shall direct our own lives."[8]

—The new government of Ukraine, immediately after declaring independence in 1918.

The United States and other western Allies formally recognized the new Ukraine National Republic in 1918. Lenin, now in control of the Russian government, also recognized the independent nation, but it was clear that he intended Ukraine to be part of Russia. He sent a letter addressing "the workers and peasants of Ukraine" and calling for a "*voluntary* union of nations—a union that would not permit coercion of one nation by another."[9]

The Government's Collapse

The excitement and patriotism Ukrainians felt after declaring independence did not last long. In fact, over the next four years Ukraine had four different governments—each proclaiming to be the independent Ukrainian National Republic. Historians often refer to the time between 1918 and 1921 as the "Ukrainian Civil War" because so many factions within Ukraine were warring for control of the country.

Around this same period, Ukraine was also the scene of continued fighting between Lenin's Bolshevik Army and the White Army troops who were loyal to the czar and the Russian Empire. A lot of these battles were fought in the eastern part of Ukraine. Some Ukrainians strongly

Ukraine

Source: Central Intelligence Agency, "Europe: Ukraine," The World Factbook.

supported the Bolsheviks and were eager to have Ukraine join Lenin's proposed Soviet Union. On December 25, 1918, in the eastern Ukrainian city of Kharkiv, the Ukrainian Bolsheviks attempted to declare Ukraine the new Soviet Ukrainian Republic. But other Ukrainians wanted an independent state, separate from Russia. Thousands on both sides of this issue joined in the fight.

Other countries sought to take advantage of the violence and disarray within Ukraine's borders. Armies from Poland, Romania, and Czechoslovakia were eager to grab as much valuable Ukrainian territory as they could from the fledgling government. Though Ukrainians fought against the intruders, they were greatly overmatched. In all, 1.5 million Ukrainian soldiers and civilians died during these conflicts.

Ukraine's new government proved to be as ineffective as its army. The members of the Rada were mostly idealists—too young and inexperienced to carry out the task they had undertaken. Just six weeks after

The National Hero

There is no person who is as revered in Ukrainian history as an eighteenth-century poet, painter, and politician named Taras Shevchenko. Though Shevchenko was born a serf, his talent as a painter earned him a chance to go to Saint Petersburg to study, but his true passion was writing poetry. However, it was poetry that resulted in his exile.

Shevchenko's poetry was often political. He wrote about the glory days of the Cossacks and complained that after the Cossack era, Ukraine's glory days had ended. In a part of one poem written in 1844, he ridiculed the czars who had plundered Ukraine:

> It was [Peter] the First who crucified
>
> Unfortunate Ukraine
>
> And [Catherine] the Second—she who finished off
>
> Whatever yet remained.

For writing such verse critical of Russians, especially because it was so popular with Ukrainians, Shevchenko was sentenced to serve ten years in exile as a soldier in the Russian army in central Asia. Under the terms of his exile he was not allowed to paint or write. Eventually he was pardoned but was not permitted to return to his beloved Ukraine. Today Shevchenko is still revered in Ukraine for popularizing the Cossacks, and his work inspired many other Ukrainian writers, dramatists, and poets. His image is on Ukrainian currency and on numerous monuments that replaced many of the Lenin statues after Ukraine's 1991 declaration of independence.

Quoted in Paul Kubicek, *The History of Ukraine*. Westport, CT: Greenwood, 2008, p. 57.

Lenin's Bolsheviks took over Petrograd, pro-Bolshevik troops consisting of both Russians and Ukrainians marched into Kiev, says Reid, "ineffectually opposed by a scratch collection of peasants, schoolboys, and ex-prisoners of war."[10]

Soon after the Bolshevik march on Kiev the newly elected government fled to western Ukraine. They continued to pass new laws, although few of any substance and none that dealt with the pressing problems faced by the Ukrainian people. In his biography of Hrushevsky, Thomas Prymak notes, "In various obscure towns, along the railway line, laws were passed about the socialization of land, about the introduction of the New Style calendar, a new monetary system, a coat-of-arms for the Republic, [and] Ukrainian citizenship."[11]

Another Beginning

By the time the fighting in Ukraine ended in 1921, the independent nation of Ukraine no longer existed. Once again, it was divided among its more powerful neighbors. Poland had seized Galicia (an area in western Ukraine). The Czechoslovakian Republic and Romania had also acquired a few small parts of Ukraine. But the bulk of Ukraine went to the new Soviet Union after Lenin's Bolsheviks, who became known as the Red Army, marched into Kiev. By 1922 Ukraine had been declared one of the first four Soviet Socialist Republics, along with Belarus, Transcaucasia, and Russia. The Ukrainian people were about to begin a whole new chapter in a long and often difficult history.

CHAPTER TWO

The Politics of Ukraine

When Ukraine officially became the Ukrainian Soviet Socialist Republic in 1922, many Ukrainians hoped for improvements in their lives. Though all of the member states of the Union of Soviet Socialist Republics (USSR) would be governed by the Communist Party in Moscow, Vladimir Lenin announced that each individual republic would have some measure of control over its own affairs. That did not come to pass. Lenin died in 1924 and was replaced by Josef Stalin, a powerful and murderous dictator who had no intention of honoring his predecessor's promises.

Forging a Soviet Identity

Stalin's long-range goal was to transform the USSR into a nation that could successfully compete with America and European countries both industrially and militarily. He saw Ukraine as essential to fulfilling that goal. Its natural resources and fertile farmland and its vast deposits of coal, petroleum, and natural gas would be enormously valuable to the Soviet Union's growing economy and its effort to improve its standing in world affairs.

First, however, Stalin intended to eliminate any feelings of nationalism among Ukrainians. He believed that the pride and loyalty citizens felt for their native country might distract the Ukrainian people from celebrating their new identity as devoted, hardworking Soviet citizens. To erase Ukrainian nationalism, Stalin began a series of purges, killing or imprisoning people he felt were secretly working against him or who were likely to voice opposition to his ideas. Stalin's purges, for instance, labeled successful Ukrainian farmers and businessmen as political enemies. In speeches he exaggerated their wealth and stressed their selfishness, a strategy intended to gain support among the vast majority who lived much more modest lives.

"Enemies of the People"

The reality of life under Stalin was far worse than anyone had imagined. Stalin maintained control of Ukraine and all of the other Soviet republics through fear. Anyone identified as an "enemy of the people" was likely to meet with an untimely death. It barely mattered that most of the people who ended up on Stalin's enemies lists had done nothing wrong. One Kiev woman, whose grandparents were targeted during Stalin's purges of the 1930s, says the randomness of Stalin's choices of "enemies" to be purged served its purpose: Fear abounded. "You didn't have to really hide because Stalin didn't care about who was on the list and who was not on the list, it didn't matter," she tells Anna Reid. "What the Stalin regime cared about was the constant threat, the constant fear."[12]

> "You didn't have to really hide because Stalin didn't care about who was on the list and who was not on the list."[12]
>
> —Kiev woman explaining the randomness of who was chosen by Stalin to be killed during the purges of 1930s.

Stalin appointed Nikita Khrushchev as the first secretary of the Communist Party in Ukraine in 1938. Stalin believed the Ukrainian-born Khrushchev could more easily identify any members of the party who might be working against the dictator. His faith in Khrushchev was well-founded. Within six months of his appointment, Khrushchev claimed to have identified eighty-three of the eighty-six members of the Ukrainian Communist Party's Central Committee who he said had been secretly working against Stalin. Khrushchev went on to become premier of the Soviet Union in 1953, after Stalin's death.

Josef Stalin (left) and Nikita Khrushchev wave to crowds in the mid-1930s. Stalin appointed the Ukrainian-born Khrushchev as first secretary of the Communist Party; Khrushchev later succeeded Stalin as Soviet premier.

Khrushchev and the Thaw

Khrushchev had regularly enforced Stalin's brutal policies of political repression in Ukraine. Therefore his countrymen had little hope of change. However, many of their fears were calmed soon after February 25, 1956, when Khrushchev delivered a six-hour speech to a closed session of the 20th Congress of the Communist Party of the Soviet Union in Moscow. No guests or members of the press were allowed; thus, Khrushchev's address later became known as the "Secret Speech." Even so, historians say, word of Khrushchev's speech leaked very soon afterward to the Ukraine people.

In this six-hour speech Khrushchev distanced himself from Stalin by being sharply critical of his predecessor's tyrannical methods:

Stalin . . . used extreme methods and mass repression at a time when the revolution was already victorious, when the Soviet state

was strengthened, when the exploiting classes were already liquidated . . . . It is clear that here Stalin showed in a whole series of
cases his intolerance, his brutality and his abuse of power. Instead
of proving his political correctness and mobilizing the masses,
he often chose the path of repression and physical annihilation,
not only against actual enemies, but also against individuals who
had not committed any crimes against the Party and the Soviet
government.[13]

The speech signaled a thaw in Russia's dealings with its Soviet republics. But Ukrainians were skeptical; they had seen firsthand the politically motivated cruelties for which Khrushchev had been notorious
during Stalin's regime. For example, it was Khrushchev who forced an
estimated 1.5 million Poles and Jews from western Ukraine to labor
camps in Siberia and Kazakhstan. In addition, he personally carried out
Stalin's purges, overseeing the deaths of people suspected of being enemies within the party.

Despite widespread skepticism, Ukrainians noticed some positive
changes in their relationship with Moscow. For the first time since the
1920s, ethnic Ukrainians were selected to head the Communist Party of
Ukraine, and a number of political prisoners from Ukraine were released
from the *gulags*, harsh labor camps in frigid areas of northern Russia.
Finally, in a surprise move to celebrate three hundred years of Ukrainian
and Russian unification, Khrushchev transferred control of Crimea from
Russia to Ukraine. "These were merely gestures from a man who had
been very much disliked," says Yukechka, a Ukrainian woman now living in the United States. "In the minds of some people back then, even
gestures were welcome. But you see, a great many Ukraine people were
suspicious—how could they not be? It did not seem likely for a man like
him, who had been so hard on his own people, to give gifts."[14]

The Winds of Political Change

Though Ukrainians acknowledged that Khrushchev was an improvement
over Stalin, he had little interest in the idea of Ukrainian nationalism. And
the subsequent leaders of the Soviet Union were even more restrictive in

matters involving Ukraine. One of the most restrictive was Khrushchev's protégé, Leonid Brezhnev, who replaced Khrushchev in 1964.

Brezhnev's stern approach was evident when he appointed his good friend Volodymyr Shcherbytsky as the head of Ukraine's Communist Party. Shcherbytsky wanted to make Ukraine a model of what communism could achieve. However, his vision of the way Ukraine should be governed was far more repressive than Khrushchev's had been. Under Shcherbytsky, political changes that Khrushchev had enacted were cancelled. According to political science professor Paul Kubicek, Shcherbytsky was quick to crack down on dissenters. "Activists were monitored by the secret police; some lost their academic or cultural positions; many were arrested."[15] Included among the arrests were Ukraine Communist Party members who dared to criticize the government. With the arrests came more purges that sent additional "enemies" to the gulags.

Gorbachev's Reforms

Ukrainians found Mikhail Gorbachev a welcome contrast to Brezhnev when he became president in 1985. Though Gorbachev was a firm believer in the economic goals and ideals of communism, he opposed the repressive tactics of his predecessors. Gorbachev promised to institute new policies that he hoped would lead to changes that would make the Soviet Union stronger—both economically and politically. For example, he believed that *demokratizatsiia*—democratization—would give people more of a say in elections. Though Ukrainians and other Soviet citizens had been allowed to vote, there usually had been just one name on the ballot for each office. Under *demokratizatsiia* voters would have a choice between candidates for each office; however, only the Communist Party was represented. A vote that amounted to less than 50 percent for a particular candidate was considered a "no confidence" vote, and the party would choose another candidate to run. By allowing choices of candidates, Gorbachev hoped that more progressives who favored reform would be elected, thus making his government stronger.

Gorbachev also instituted a policy of *glasnost,* which translates as both "tolerance" and "openness." He believed that the Soviet Union

Purges and Political Enemies

Many of the Ukrainians targeted for purges were not killed immediately but rather were sentenced to work for a number of years in what was known as the gulag, a system of forced labor camps. Many of these camps were located in the coldest, most remote parts of Russia. Most of the prisoners died of hunger, exhaustion, or cold long before their sentences were fulfilled.

One of the camps, called Kolyma, was a massive complex that housed more than one hundred thousand prisoners at a time. Inmates at Kolyma worked in the gold fields, digging in temperatures that often reached -58°F (-50°C). For this heavy, grueling work, prisoners were fed 28 ounces of bread (794 g) and a few ounces of fish per day. Those who did not meet the desired daily quota had their food portions reduced. A prisoner that surpassed the quota of gold for the day—quite rare—might receive a bonus of a tiny bottle of cheap cologne to drink (because it contained alcohol, it was warming).

More likely, prisoners became so weak from either illness or lack of food that they could not meet their quotas. Subsequently these unfortunate souls had their rations cut, making them even weaker and less likely to meet their quotas. According to historical records, about 3 million prisoners died at Kolyma between 1932 and 1954.

would be a stronger nation by allowing and even encouraging citizens to voice their opinions. He also urged that glasnost be expanded to apply to the news media, resulting in a freer dissemination of news and information to the public. Kubicek notes that glasnost "would give [Gorbachev] a weapon—an invigorated press—with which he could combat corrupt and more conservative elements within the Communist Party."[16]

Ironically, Gorbachev's reforms proved to be damaging to his presidency—especially within Ukraine. Allowed for the first time to speak openly, Ukrainians became more and more vocal about their dissatisfaction with political, economic, and social conditions in their country. Among the issues that got the most attention was the government's handling of the 1986 Chernobyl nuclear accident. The Chernobyl nuclear power plant in Ukraine, 60 miles (96.5 km) north of Kiev, experienced a catastrophic event on April 27, 1986. One of the plant's four nuclear reactors exploded, releasing tons of dangerous radioactive material into the atmosphere.

Though the government knew about the accident, officials chose not to acknowledge the explosion right away or to warn people about the health emergency. That lack of candor by the government infuriated Ukrainians, and many blamed Gorbachev. "The horrible way they handled Chernobyl did it, not telling the Ukraine people about it for days and days—it was like the dam had broken," says Ukrainian émigré Sergei Karastov. "All of that anger and frustration, and now people could release it—and Gorbachev and his government were the main targets."[17]

> "All of that anger and frustration, and now people could release it—and Gorbachev and his government were the main targets."[17]
>
> —Émigré Sergei Karastov on the failure of Gorbachev's policy of glasnost.

Calls for Freedom

By September 1989 some of the loudest voices of protest against Gorbachev's presidency came from a new Ukrainian political organization called *Rukh* (the Russian word for "movement"). Rukh had been formed partly in response to the government's handling of the Chernobyl accident, but Rukh's main goal was Ukrainian independence. The organization staged sit-ins and hunger strikes and even mobilized a half million people to create a 50-mile-long (80.4 km) human chain connecting the Ukrainian cities of Kiev and L'viv. Rukh persisted in its demands, and in 1991 Rukh was allowed to register as a political party. In an election held that year, more than one hundred Rukh candidates won seats in the Ukrainian legislature.

The election of pro-democracy candidates was an important first step toward Ukraine's efforts to sever ties with the Soviet Union. But chaos

Under Mikhail Gorbachev, Ukrainians publicly expressed their anger at the Soviet government's handling of the 1986 Chernobyl nuclear power plant accident. The ruined Chernobyl reactor is pictured, twenty years after the accident.

occurred in August 1991 when hard-line Communists tried to oust Gorbachev from office. Though the move did not succeed, it demonstrated how disorganized and weak the Soviet government had become. Soon after the attempted coup, on August 24, 1991, Ukraine took advantage of the mayhem in Moscow and declared its independence from the Soviet Union.

Organizing a New Government

Once Ukraine had declared its independence it had to decide how to organize a new government. As a Soviet republic, Ukraine's laws and government structure had been created entirely by the Soviet Union. The country's military had been equipped and led by Soviet leaders, and foreign relations had been entirely in the hands of the Soviet president in

The Tragedy of Chernobyl

The explosion at the Chernobyl nuclear plant occurred just after 1 a.m. on April 27, 1986. It released ten tons of radioactive material into the atmosphere—four hundred times more powerful than the atomic bomb dropped on Hiroshima in World War II, and fourteen times greater than the 2012 Fukushima nuclear disaster in Japan.

For days, however, the Soviet government said nothing about what had happened. In fact, not until scientists at a Swedish nuclear facility noticed the nuclear cloud on their radar two days later did the Soviets acknowledge the explosion. However, their announcement downplayed any dangers to human health. And it was not until two weeks after that that Gorbachev appeared on television to explain the scale of the damage.

Thirty-one people died almost immediately—some burned to death fighting the fires or trying to escape. Tens of thousands more have died in the decades since from radioactive poisoning or have become sickened by cancers caused by their exposure to the radioactive particles. Experts say many of these deaths and illnesses could have been avoided if the government had immediately told Ukrainian citizens what had happened. "Ask a Ukrainian when he stopped believing in communism," says Anna Reid, "and the answers vary. . . . But by far the likeliest reply is 'Chernobyl.' . . . the Chernobyl affair epitomized everything that was wrong with the Soviet Union."

Anna Reid, *Borderland: A Journey Through the History of Ukraine*, Boulder, CO: Westview, 2000, p. 194.

Moscow. Thus the challenge was to create a new government by and for Ukraine—a government that would decide everything from how to pass new laws to how often elections should be held.

Under Ukraine's constitution, ratified in 1996, the new government consisted of a president, a 450-member legislature called the *Verkhovna Rada*, (sometimes just called the Rada), and a supreme court. Ukrainian citizens aged eighteen and older had the privilege of voting for a president and for Rada representatives. A president would be elected to serve a five-year term and would be eligible to run for a second term. The most important jobs of the president consisted of commanding Ukraine's armed forces and appointing a cabinet of ministers who would oversee agriculture, commerce, and foreign affairs. The prime minister of Ukraine was the head of the cabinet.

The first Ukrainian president was Leonid Kravchuk, a former leader of Ukraine's Communist Party. Though Kravchuk had agreed to work with Rukh leaders and other pro-democracy advocates, little changed during his administration or during the administration of his successor, Leonid Kuchma. Instead, many charges of wrongdoing surfaced; these included bribery and payoffs, illegal arms sales to Iraq during dictator Saddam Hussein's regime, and even the beheading of a journalist critical of Kuchma's administration. Many began to wonder whether an uncorrupted democratic government was even possible in Ukraine.

Troubling Elections

One of the biggest challenges of governing Ukraine was the wide split between pro-Russian Ukrainians in the east and pro-West Ukrainians in west and central Ukraine. And no event demonstrated this difficulty more clearly than the presidential election of 2004. The candidate favored by the pro-Russian voting bloc was Viktor Yanukovych, who had served as Kuchma's prime minister. His challenger was Viktor Yushchenko, a pro-West candidate who was popular with voters in central and western Ukraine. However, just before the first round of the elections, Yushchenko became gravely ill soon after dining with a member of Ukraine's secret police.

Hospital tests proved that Yushchenko had been poisoned with a very high dose of a chemical called dioxin. Most people have a tiny amount of dioxin in their bloodstream from years of breathing polluted air or eating produce that has been treated with certain chemicals. But tests revealed that Yushchenko's dioxin levels were six thousand times the amount commonly found in humans. Yushchenko survived, although the dioxin caused painful sores in his internal organs as well as a grayish skin tone and masses of scars and skin lesions that bloated and disfigured his face.

Furious, Yushchenko publicly accused his political rival of poisoning him. As the election neared, reports from foreign election monitors indicated other dirty tricks committed by Yanukovych supporters. Reports of fraud—including setting ballot boxes on fire and physical threats against Yushchenko voters—were widespread. Predictably, the state-controlled television and radio stations that had endorsed Yanukovych chose not to report those violations, and on November 23, 2004, Yanukovych was declared the winner.

The Orange Revolution

That election resulted in a storm of protest later known as the Orange Revolution (named after the color of Yushchenko's campaign banners). The Orange Revolution was termed by one Ukrainian expert as "the most dra-

Orange-clad supporters of opposition presidential candidate Viktor Yushchenko rally in front of Kiev's parliament in 2004. Fueled by charges of a rigged election, protesters pushed for a no-confidence vote on the election results.

matic event in Ukraine since the country achieved political independence in 1991."[18] Millions of protesters took to the streets in cities and towns throughout Ukraine to show their anger at what they believed was a rigged election and the attempted murder of Yushchenko. The demonstrators also voiced their impatience for political and economic reforms that had been promised over the years by past presidents.

The most visible protests took place in the large square in Kiev immediately after the announcement of Yanukovych's victory. The more than five hundred thousand protesters gathered there were wearing orange ribbons and waving orange flags as well as the blue and yellow flag of Ukraine. "We appeal to citizens of Ukraine to support the national resistance movement," Yushchenko told his cheering supporters. "We should not leave this square until we secure victory."[19]

The protests achieved their goal. City councils throughout many large cities in Ukraine announced a vote of no confidence in the election results. A runoff election was held, and Yushchenko emerged as the winner. He was sworn in as Ukrainian president on January 10, 2005. Ukrainians were elated that their protest had succeeded.

> "We appeal to citizens of Ukraine to support the national resistance movement. We should not leave this square until we secure victory."[19]
>
> —Presidential candidate Viktor Yushchenko, during the Orange Revolution.

Yanukovych Returns

However optimistic the Ukrainian people had been after the Orange Revolution, Yushchenko's presidency was a disappointment. Charges of corruption arose almost from the beginning of his term. His longtime friend Petro Poroshenko, who had been named as head of the National Security and Defense Council, resigned after being accused of accepting bribes. In April 2005 Yushchenko's minister of justice admitted that the academic records he had submitted as part of his résumé were fraudulent. Yushchenko's family was not immune to hints of corruption, either. Voters were outraged when it was made public that Yushchenko's nineteen-year-old son possessed a $40,000 platinum cell phone and lived in a luxury apartment.

Yushchenko quickly lost much of his political support, and after his five-year term was up in 2009, the voters chose Yanukovych by a narrow margin in the presidential race.

But Yanukovych's presidency became contentious when the question of alliances came up. At first he agreed to join the European Union, a federation made up of twenty-eight countries banded together in economic and political policy. But in late 2013 Yanukovych changed his mind and expressed his intent to establish closer ties with Russia instead. Outraged Ukrainians took to the streets, demanding that Yanukovych either reverse his decision or resign.

By December 2013 more than 1 million Ukrainians had joined the protests against Yanukovych in the *Maidan* in Kiev. By February 2014 Yanukovych was being accused of improper use of government funds to furnish his luxurious country estate, as well as using the police force to intimidate political rivals and critics. He fled Ukraine a week later, and Ukraine's Parliament declared Yanukovych unable to fulfill his duties as president and scheduled a new election for May 2014.

CHAPTER THREE

The Economy of Ukraine

When Ukraine joined the Soviet Union in 1922 Lenin knew how valuable the new republic's resources would be. Ukraine had large deposits of coal, aluminum, titanium, graphite, and marble. Gold, gemstones, and natural gas reserves also lay in abundance under the Ukrainian soil. But it was the farmland that was of prime importance in the early days of the Soviet Union. Soviet leaders saw Ukraine's fertile soil as an important source of food for the entire Soviet Union.

An Unpopular Economic Idea

Before Ukraine became a Soviet republic, most of the country's farmland was owned by individual farmers, or peasants. This was supposed to change under communism, which aimed to do away with private property—transferring ownership of all factories and farms to the state. Once this change took place, people who worked on farms or in factories were to be paid in grain and shelter. Under communism, all workers were supposed to share equally in the results of their labor.

Lenin knew that the peasants in Ukraine had suffered a great deal during the civil war. Rather than deal aggressively with them, he temporarily postponed his new farm policy. Instead, his New Economic Policy (NEP) of March 1921 focused first on collectivizing banks and shoring up political support for communism in urban areas. Lenin tried to calm Bolshevik concerns about concessions made to the peasants by noting, "We are engaged in a strategic retreat that will allow us to advance on a broad front in the very near future."[20]

Stalin's Five-Year Plan

All of this changed with Lenin's death in 1924. His successor, Josef Stalin, had no interest in continuing Lenin's gradual changeover to a Communist economy. In 1928 Stalin instituted a Five-Year Plan that set two ambitious goals. One was for the Soviet Union to achieve rapid industrialization, a process that required the building of factories and hydroelectric dams and expanding the nation's mining capabilities. Because Ukraine had so much coal and natural gas, most of the industrial expansion would take place there. In fact, plans called for more than four hundred new industrial plants to be built in Ukraine between 1928 and 1932.

But achieving Stalin's goal of industrialization would require a lot of money. That money was to come from the collectivization of farms—the most immediate goal. There were 25 million farms throughout the Soviet Union, a large number of which were in Ukraine. Stalin planned to combine large numbers of small family farms into huge collective farms, worked by the peasants and monitored by state officials. According to writer Ryan Ver Berkmoes, Stalin wanted to try collectivization in Ukraine first because he considered Ukraine "a laboratory for testing Soviet restructuring, while stamping out harmful nationalism."[21]

Once collectivization was under way the state could sell grain and other crops and use the profits to purchase machinery for the nation's industrial growth. Stalin insisted that haste was vital in improving the Soviet economy. Russia's economy, he said, had long suffered from neglect, which in turn had left the country far behind other nations and would spell disaster if it continued. "One feature of the history of old Russia was the continual beating she suffered because of her backwardness," Stalin said in a February 1931 speech. "We are fifty or a hundred years behind the advanced countries. We must make good this distance in ten years. Either we do it, or we shall be crushed."[22]

> "One feature of the history of old Russia was the continual beating she suffered because of her backwardness."[22]
>
> —Josef Stalin, on the importance of collectivizing farms and improving the economy.

Hostility Toward Collectivization

Collectivization was no more popular with peasants than it had been years before when Lenin had first introduced it. Ukraine's peasants were vehement critics of collectivization. Approximately 86 percent of Ukrainians lived in rural areas, most on small farms. They had owned their small plots of lands for many years, as had their fathers and grandfathers before them. They had no desire to work on government-owned collective farms, known as *kolkhozy*.

When Communist officials came to their villages to seize the farms, livestock, and machinery to begin organizing the *kolkhozy*, many peasants rebelled. Rather than turn over their livestock, they killed their own animals—butchering chickens, hogs, cattle, and even horses so the government could not have them. Many also destroyed their own machinery for the same reason.

Members of a Soviet collective farm load their harvest on a truck headed to market. Stalin forced small, private farms in Ukraine and elsewhere to join together in government-run collective farms.

Ways to find Hidden Grain

In his book *Execution by Hunger: The Hidden Holocaust*, Miron Dolot shares his personal experiences as a boy living through Stalin's famine of 1932–1933 in Ukraine. In the following excerpt Dolot describes how far Stalin's commissions of Communist officials went to find any hidden grain on the farms of the starving peasants.

> The commission went from house to house, day and night, searching for "hidden bread." Each commission had its experts for this purpose. The experts responsible for searching for grain in the ground were equipped with special screw-type rods. The long rods sharpened at one end were used for probing haystacks or tacks of straw, and the thatched roofs of the farmers' houses. The commission members searched everywhere: They drilled holes in the gardens, backyards, in the earth floors of the houses, and in the farm buildings. They looked for grain under beds, in the lattices and cellars. They never missed checking inside the stoves and ovens, on and under shelves, in trunks, and up in the chimneys. They measured the thickness of the walls, and inspected them for bulges where grain could have been concealed. . . . Nothing in the houses remained intact or untouched. They upturned everything, even the cribs of babies, and even babies themselves were thoroughly frisked. . . . Even the smallest amount that was found was confiscated.

Miron Dolot, *Execution by Hunger: The Hidden Holocaust*. New York: W.W. Norton, 1987, pp. 166–67.

Ridding the Country of *Kulaks*

Stalin was furious with these actions; he accused Ukraine's farmers of trying to derail his Five-Year Plan. He called any farmer who dared to speak out against collectivization a greedy *kulak*—a Russian word that referred to farmers who were considered to be somewhat prosperous.

For instance, they might own two cows rather than one, or they might hire a worker or two during busy harvest time rather than do all of the work themselves. Stalin, however, meant it as a derogatory term—a label that would ostracize those farmers who dared oppose his plans. Kulaks were depicted as selfish enemies of the state who wanted more than their fair share and who, for the sake of the rest of the population, must be eliminated.

One of the most frequently used slogans in the Soviet Union in the late 1920s and early 1930s was: "Those who do not join the *kolkhoz* are enemies of soviet power. The heroic period of our socialist construction has arrived. The kulaks must be liquidated."[23] Toward this end, Stalin ordered the seizure of all kulak farms in Ukraine. After being evicted the peasants were either shot or loaded onto freight cars and exiled to work in the gulags. Altogether, more than 1.8 million Ukrainian peasants died of cold, starvation, or disease during the years of collectivization.

Violence in the Countryside

Even as Stalin was carrying out "dekulakization" in Ukraine, he was counting on those same farms to produce massive amounts of grain. The Communist planning agency Gosplan had previously determined that selling 7.7 million tons of grain each year on the international market was necessary to finance the nation's industrial growth as well as build up the Soviet military. Many Communist leaders in Ukraine believed that goal was unrealistic because of the chaos caused by the new farming system and resistance to it. Even so, Stalin insisted that peasants intensify their efforts to meet that goal.

It was a doomed effort. In 1932, when Stalin learned that the yield would fall far short of the goal, he orchestrated a punishment against the peasants. First he sealed Ukraine's borders so no one could leave, and then he starved them to death. The famine that Stalin set upon Ukraine is known as the *Holodomor*, or Great Hunger. Between 1932 and 1933 Stalin's police forces and Communist Party officials stormed the countryside, seizing crops, stores of grain, and seeds set aside for the next planting. With nothing to eat, peasants starved. Whole families and then

In 2013 Ukrainians lit candles to mark the memory of victims of the Holodomor, *the 1930s famine orchestrated by Stalin. Stalin devised the famine to punish Ukraine's peasant farmers for falling short of crop goals.*

entire villages simply disappeared. One Ukrainian survivor later recalled: "Stalin took everything from the people. The result was starvation—people were falling in the street. It is too sad to talk about. By 1933 all was gone and people were forced to go to the collective farm. They took everything. My sister was asking my mother for something to eat, but there was no milk or bread. My sister wanted to eat her hands, so my mother tied her hands to her side."[24]

The famine that resulted from Stalin's collectivization in Ukraine resulted in the deaths of between 6 million and 8 million men, women, and children. In 1933 one of Stalin's lieutenants insisted that the famine was a great success. It showed the peasants, he said, "who is the master here. It cost millions of lives, but the collective farm system is here to stay."[25]

The Post-Stalin Economy

Stalin died in 1953, and his successors were far less aggressive in their economic policies. But while they did not levy punishing taxes or other requirements against the Ukrainian people, they did little to stabilize Ukraine's shaky economy.

Nikita Khrushchev, who became leader of the USSR in 1953, recognized that the Soviet economy was faltering. He believed that the centralized economy, where all decision making emanated from Moscow, was partly to blame. In an effort to improve economic output, Khrushchev allowed Ukraine and the other Soviet republics to establish their own economic councils. The idea was that a local council would be more familiar with the particular needs of the republic and therefore would make better financial decisions. Khrushchev also funneled more government money into the Soviet agricultural sector, allowing the collectives to buy more supplies and machinery, which was some help to Ukraine's struggling farmers. However, Ukraine's economy remained sluggish, as did the economies of the other Soviet republics.

> "Stalin took everything from the people. The result was starvation—people were falling in the street. It is too sad to talk about."[24]
>
> —A survivor of the famine of 1932–1933.

When Khrushchev died in 1964 Leonid Brezhnev succeeded him. Historians say that in his eighteen years in office, Brezhnev was far more interested in shoring up his own political power than in enacting economic reforms. He reversed Khrushchev's reforms, restoring centralized economic decision making to Moscow. During Brezhnev's regime, which lasted until 1972, frequent shortages of food and clothing plagued residents of Ukraine and the other Soviet republics.

Perestroika and Mikhail Gorbachev

In 1985 Mikhail Gorbachev became leader of the USSR and proved to be a different sort of leader from his predecessors. Gorbachev knew that something needed to change in the USSR's troubled economy. Goods produced in the USSR tended to be of poor quality, and the economy as a whole, he believed, was poorly managed. A large part of the problem, he felt, was the years-old rivalry between the United States and the Soviet Union. In what was termed the "Cold War," both sides had spent millions of dollars to develop nuclear weapons. That arms race, Gorbachev believed, was draining money from the Soviet economy.

In 1986 he introduced perestroika, a plan for restructuring the Soviet economy. Under perestroika, workers in Ukraine as well as other Soviet Republics would be able to have limited ownership of businesses and property, giving people a greater incentive to work hard. Gorbachev believed that the best, most lasting economic reforms were likely to come from the bottom of the employment chain. Instead of having Moscow make all the decisions for businesses and factories, under perestroika the managers and workers would be given the authority to decide what worked best for them.

But Gorbachev's ideas were met with hostility by many Communist leaders, especially Volodymyr Shcherbytsky, the head of Ukraine's Communist Party. Shcherbytsky was certain that if implemented, Gorbachev's reforms would undermine one of communism's basic ideas: that the government—not individuals—should have the power to make all economic decisions.

By 1991, however, the Soviet Union was already in decline. The disaster at Chernobyl had been horribly mismanaged by Gorbachev and his advisers. The reforms that had been the cornerstone of Gorbachev's administration had not materialized—and Ukraine was ready to declare its independence.

An Undecided Free Ukraine

One of Ukraine's first goals after declaring independence on August 24, 1991, was to determine the type of economy the new country would have. Many hoped that Ukraine would adopt a free-market economy in which businesses decide for themselves what to produce and sell and what to charge rather than rely on the government to make these choices. In addition, business owners would determine how best to market their products

Ukraine's Shadow Economy

Ukraine's economy is often referred to as a "shadow economy" because much of it involves people making money through illegal activities such as bribery and smuggling. Another part of the shadow economy that is posing problems for Ukraine is the prevalence of what are called "envelope salaries"—employers paying their workers in cash rather than paychecks. In fact, Ukraine's prime minister reported at the end of 2012 that about 29 percent of Ukrainians were working under this type of arrangement.

It is a cheaper method for employers because they do not have to pay taxes to the government for every payroll check. And employees like the system because they do not have taxes withheld from paychecks. The problem for Ukraine's government, however, is significant. An unbelievable $21.26 billion in salaries are paid unofficially, so the state does not get its share of tax revenue, which experts say amounts to between $11 billion and $12 billion each year. That revenue is needed to fix roads, build bridges, invest in education and reform programs, and shore up the struggling economy.

However, many experts say Ukrainians are unlikely to embrace new regulations against envelope salaries. "I can tell you that I have my doubts people will pay taxes faithfully," says Oleksand Garan, a political science professor in Kiev. "There is a very low trust in everything: banking system, pension fund, tax system, [and] government. . . . Do you really think that if someone has a chance to save some money he will go to report real taxes? I doubt it."

Quoted in forUM, "Income Declarations in Ukraine: Straight Dealing Does Not Hide?," June 12, 2013. http://en.for-ua.com.

and how much to pay their employees. No one would have a guaranteed job or a guaranteed rate of pay; hiring and pay would depend on business needs, which in turn would be based on whatever the market could bear.

But the process of making the transition from a government-run economy to a free-market system is neither easy nor quick, as Ukraine soon learned. Not all Ukrainians were eager to adopt a free-market economy, for it involved risks. Under the Communist system, people often had little or no chance of advancement and lacked the ability to pursue a career of their own choosing. But they were generally guaranteed a job and a certain level of pay. These are not guaranteed in a free-market system. That lack of predictability frightened some Ukrainians. What is more, many in eastern Ukraine wanted to maintain strong economic ties with Russia. Some even proposed that Russia and Ukraine form an economic partnership.

Struggling for Money

Ukraine's free-market economy had problems almost from the start. In the 1990s runaway inflation was the biggest problem facing Ukrainian families. By 1994 the inflation rate hit an almost unheard-of 10,000 percent. Rising prices of goods, coupled with layoffs and high unemployment rates, resulted in hardship for millions of Ukrainians. Food, clothing, and other necessities were simply too expensive for many families.

Consumers were not the only ones hurting. Many companies laid off workers, while others simply went bankrupt. Still other companies, reluctant to close, opted to pay their workers with goods instead of cash. "Workers were 'paid in kind,'" explains Paul Kubicek, "meaning in lieu of wages they received products (e.g., sausages, clothing, toilet paper) produced by their place of employment and then were expected to resell these products to generate cash or other necessities."[26]

Many of these employees were so strapped for money that they resorted to what is known as "suitcase trading." That involved carrying oversized luggage filled with such goods across the border into Poland, Russia, or Romania to sell at a profit. Some of these suitcase traders would cross the border ten or more times each year. And while suitcase trading was illegal, hundreds of thousands of Ukrainians were desperate enough to engage in the practice. Ukraine's economy had become so dysfunctional in the 1990s, Kubicek notes, "that the verb to 'Ukrainianize' acquired in the Russian language the meaning 'to bring to ruin.'"[27]

Cars drive over large potholes on a road near Ukraine's capital city of Kiev in 2013. The country's infrastructure of roads, bridges, and railways has suffered because of ongoing economic difficulties.

Strikes and Shortages

Even though they often were not paid regularly during this time, many employees continued to work, assured by their employers that they would eventually be paid. By November 1995 coal miners had not been paid in eight months. More than one hundred thousand miners from twenty-one mines in eastern Ukraine's Donets Basin went on strike. In addition, twenty-four miners staged a ten-day hunger strike at the office of the Coal Industry Minister, hoping to call attention to the miners' difficulties. Though Ukraine was no longer Communist, its economy was slow to privatize the coal industry, so it was still controlled by the government. Workers were frustrated by stagnant (or unpaid) wages, while consumers were angry because of the shortages of goods and services that they needed.

Energy shortages were a primary source of frustration for businesses, too. Manufacturers had been especially hurt by the high price of natural gas, which Ukraine depends on for producing electricity and running factories. Before the 2004 elections in which the pro-West Viktor Yushchenko was elected president of Ukraine, the Russian gas company Gazprom supplied natural gas to Ukraine at only about one-fifth the price other European countries paid. Since that time, however, Gazprom has increased the price to the level it charged the rest of the world—a price that has continued to hobble Ukraine's economy.

A Crumbling Infrastructure

An infrastructure in need of repair is one of the most important causes of Ukraine's current economic difficulties. Bridges, railways, and especially the nation's highways are so damaged that many manufacturers have trouble getting their goods to market. That is especially problematic for perishable goods, such as fruits and vegetables, which often rot even before they get to grocery stores. "Unless you've seen it, you wouldn't believe the condition of Ukraine's roads," says William Smyth, who has spent a great deal of time in Ukraine doing humanitarian work. "I've seen potholes so wide and so deep that they've swallowed an entire car, breaking axles and everything. If the Ukrainian government is really serious about getting their economy where it needs to be, repairing its infrastructure needs to be job number one."[28] Ukraine's economy has been mostly agricultural, but that is changing in the twenty-first century. Ukrainian factories manufacture cars and trucks, and workers mine coal and iron ore. However, in 2014 the greatest worry for Ukraine's economy is the nation's energy dependence. More than 75 percent of Ukraine's natural gas and oil and all of its nuclear fuel are imported—mostly from Russia. But because of ongoing conflicts with Russia, a steady supply of vital energy supplies from that country is in jeopardy—as is Ukraine's economy.

> "I've seen potholes so wide and so deep that they've swallowed an entire car."[28]
>
> —William Smyth, frequent visitor to Ukraine, on the nation's highways.

46

CHAPTER FOUR

The Social Fabric of Ukraine

A great deal of damage was done to the culture and social structure of Ukraine during its time as a Soviet republic. Almost every aspect of social life—from language and music to books, newspapers, and even public health—was negatively affected during Soviet rule. In some cases the damage is ongoing. But in other instances Ukrainians are moving forward with positive results.

The Strategy of *Korenizatsiya*

Lenin's goal was to spread communism throughout the world, but he realized it was crucial to make the system as appealing as possible. He knew that communism would almost certainly meet with resistance in Ukraine. Many Ukrainians were independent farmers who were set in their ways and were likely to resent drastic cultural change. And if Ukrainians rejected communism, Lenin knew it would be difficult to institute in other locations.

To make the transition to communism more appealing to the Ukrainians, Lenin implemented a system called *korenizatsiya*, or "putting down roots." In effect, *korenizatsiya* encouraged the large non-Russian population in Ukraine and throughout the Soviet Union to keep their own languages and customs, especially as their political and economic system was changing. This was a reversal of the policy enacted by the czars that changed the official language of any newly conquered territory to Russian.

In Ukraine, *korenizatsiya* resulted in Ukrainian being the primary language used in virtually all aspects of daily life, including government and education. Newspapers and books, road signs, and official publications were all published in Ukrainian. In addition, hundreds of Ukrainian-language schools were established throughout the republic in the mid-1920s. Thousands of Ukrainians who had grown up speaking Russian were finally able to learn the language of their ancestors.

Perhaps the most significant aspect of *korenizatsiya* was the government-sponsored celebration of the work of Ukrainian artists, writers, poets, musicians, and scholars. In her book *Borderland: A Journey Through the History of Ukraine*, Anna Reid tells of Ukrainian Petro Hryhorenko, an officer in the Soviet army, who was introduced in the mid-1920s to his native culture under *korenizatsiya*. The teachers gave him a newfound pride in the culture of his ancestors. During this period, he writes, "[I] first saw and heard played the Ukrainian national musical instrument, the *bandore*. From them [the teachers] I learned of *Kobzar*, [a book of poems] written by the great Ukrainian poet Taras Grigoryevich Shevchenko. And from them I learned that I belonged to the same nationality as the great Shevchenko, that I was Ukrainian."[29]

Killing the Culture

Ukraine's experience with *korenizatsiya* was short-lived; it ended soon after Lenin's death when Stalin came to power. In 1928 Stalin not only reinstated Russian as the Soviet Union's official language but also went further by banning any use of Ukrainian words or phrases. Stalin sought to solidify the Soviet identity by eliminating all reminders of individual cultures and languages. Within weeks of Stalin's announcements, the Ukrainian language schools that had opened under Lenin were closed. All Soviet leaders—many of whom had worked hard to learn Ukrainian under previous orders from Moscow—were required to start conducting all government business in Russian. Violating the rules would result in being imprisoned or being exiled for years of slave labor.

But this was just the beginning of Stalin's plan for Ukraine and the other Soviet republics. The Ukrainian literature, art, and music that had

To make the transition to communism more appealing, Lenin urged Ukrainians to celebrate their culture's artists and writers. This is how many Ukrainians learned about Taras Grigoryevich Shevchenko (pictured), whose work is considered central to modern Ukrainian literature.

been celebrated under Lenin was banned under Stalin, and many of the artists, writers, and musicians were killed or imprisoned. Theater groups and journalists suffered a similar fate; many were killed or exiled after being added to Stalin's long list of enemies considered a threat to the Soviet state.

Killing the Music

One of the aspects of the culture that was particularly popular was the music of Ukraine's blind minstrels, who were known as the *kobzari*. These musicians were poor and lived by getting alms, or donations, from listeners when they played. They accompanied themselves on traditional Ukrainian instruments such as the *kobza*—a kind of lute—and the *lira*, which is similar to a hurdy-gurdy or wheel fiddle (which is a stringed instrument played by turning a crank that rubs against strings to produce music).

Kobzari traveled from village to village, attracting large crowds with their songs of Ukraine's past and present. Soviet leaders worried about the effect of such songs on the population. Notes one cultural historian of Ukraine, "The Soviet regime feared that these traveling musicians could spread anti-Communist, religious, and ethnic propaganda and that their village performances could not be controlled from above [by the government]."[30]

To prevent the *kobzari's* music from undermining the Soviet agenda, Stalin invited them to a special conference to be held in December 1933 in the Ukrainian city of Kharkiv. The *kobzari* would be interviewed and their music studied, Stalin said, to preserve it for future generations. The conference was a cruel ploy. Approximately three hundred of the *kobzari* who had assembled in Kharkiv were taken to a gully outside of the city and left to die of exposure in the bitter cold.

Religion in Soviet Ukraine

Another aspect of the lives of Ukrainians that changed dramatically under Stalin's rule was religion. At the time of the Soviet takeover, most Ukrainians were Christians who belonged to the Orthodox Church. The country also had large Catholic and Jewish populations, most of whom lived in the biggest cities. In Crimea, one-fourth of the population were Tatars—Muslims who were the descendants of Mongolians who had come to the Crimean peninsula in the thirteenth century.

But one of the key tenets of communism says that the state is the most powerful, important entity. And because religions believe that God

The Limits of a Language

At first Lenin's celebration of the Ukrainian language as part of *koreni-zatsiya* sounded like a positive step. However, it soon became clear that in the time since Ukrainian had been banned by the Russian czars, it had become inadequate and inappropriate for use in certain educational situations. Viktor Kravchenko, an aeronautics student in Kharkiv, Ukraine, during the 1920s, later recalled later how the sudden switch to Ukrainian from Russian impacted him and his fellow students at the university:

> Another dimension of confusion was added to our life in the Institute soon after I entered by an order that all instruction and examinations be conducted in the Ukraine language, not in Russian. The order applied to all schools and institutions. It was Moscow's supreme concession to the nationalist yearnings of the largest non-Russian Soviet Republic.
>
> In theory, we Ukrainians in the student body should have been pleased. In practice we were as distressed by the innovation as the non-Ukrainian minority. Even those who, like myself, had spoken Ukrainian from childhood, were not accustomed to its use as a medium of study. Several of our best professors were utterly demoralized by the linguistic switch-over. Worst of all, our local tongue simply had not caught up with modern knowledge; its vocabulary was unsuited to the purposes of electrotechnics, chemistry, aerodynamics, physics and most other sciences.

Quoted in Anna Reid, *Borderland: A Journey Through the History of Ukraine.* Boulder, CO: Westview, 2000, pp. 118–19.

is all-powerful, Stalin strictly forbade the practice of any religion. Historians say that his distaste for religion was also political—he had been furious with leaders of the Orthodox Church for aligning themselves with the czars during the Bolshevik revolution.

In 1926 Stalin announced that anyone attending services at a church, synagogue, or mosque would be tried and imprisoned. Baptisms and other religious ceremonies were strictly forbidden; weddings and funerals could take place but without any prayers or other religious observances. In many cases church elders were arrested, and religious icons and symbols (even church bells) were confiscated. The churches were then turned into granaries.

The loss of churches, synagogues, and mosques was wrenching. One Communist Party official reported hearing an elderly man say, "They've taken everything from us. They've left us nothing. Now they are removing our last comfort. Where shall we turn for comfort in our sorrows?"[31]

A 1920s-era Orthodox Church and cemetery in the Ukrainian countryside got little use during Stalin's regime. Stalin banned the practice of religion and imprisoned anyone who tried to attend church services.

World War II and Ukraine

Already reeling from Stalin's imposed famine, Ukrainians suffered further devastation during World War II. Approximately 5.5 million Ukrainians, or one-sixth of the population, died in the war. Ukraine's death count was more than that of any other European nation during the war.

Before the start of the war Stalin and Adolf Hitler had signed a secret pact to attack Poland and split the territory between them. This pact was a non-aggression treaty, meaning that neither army would attack the other and they would support one another in case of an attack by an outside force. Hitler invaded Poland from the west on September 1, 1939—an act that began World War II. On September 17 Stalin's Soviet army invaded from the east. Stalin was pleased with the result, claiming the part of Poland that had once been western Ukraine.

In 1941, after conquering most of Western Europe, Hitler shocked Stalin by breaking their non-aggression treaty and invading Ukraine. Hatred for Stalin prompted Ukraine's people to cheer the arrival of Hitler's troops. They hated the Russians so much that they were hoping the Germans would drive the Soviets from Ukraine. People hung banners across the arches of bridges proclaiming, "The Ukrainian peoples thank their liberators, the brave German Army. Heil [good wishes], Adolf Hitler!"[32]

> "They've left us nothing. Now they are removing our last comfort. Where shall we turn for comfort in our sorrows?"[31]
>
> —Elderly man in rural Ukraine, watching Soviets destroy his church.

One Ukrainian later recalled how exciting it was in her village when the Germans soldiers marched in: "When the Germans came, we welcomed them with milk, bread, butter, and eggs. The village was like a paradise with Germans offering cigarettes, chocolates, all the goods that came from the West. The people could see with their own eyes that this was a different army altogether. So they put up Ukrainian flags."[33]

Ukraine Invaded

The initial euphoria over the German army's arrival ended as soon as Hitler's intentions toward Ukraine became apparent. The first official act of Eric Koch, appointed by Hitler as Ukraine's commissar, was to close every one of Ukraine's schools. "Ukrainian children need no schools," he announced. "What they'll have to learn later will be taught to them by their German masters."[34]

Like Hitler, Koch had nothing but contempt for the Slavic peoples. He believed they were "*Untermenchen*," German for "subhumans." In a March 1943 speech at a Nazi convention in Kiev, Koch explained that Ukrainian people had virtually no worth. "We are a master race," he said, "which must remember that the lowliest German worker is racially and biologically a thousand times more valuable than the population here."[35]

Early in the winter of 1941 Nazi soldiers began sending Ukrainian civilians to be *Ostarbeiters*, or "Eastern slave laborers," in armament plants and factories in Germany. Some Ukrainians protested, begging to be allowed to stay with their families. For that, German soldiers set their farms and homes on fire. A total of 1.3 million Ukrainians were forcibly transported to Germany between April and December 1942.

One survivor of that time recalls how wrenching it was to be sent away from her home and family. "One day men in black uniforms came to our home and informed my father that since I was 15 years old, I must go to work in Germany. And so it was my turn to say goodbye to my parents, to my Ukraine."[36]

> "Ukrainian children need no schools. What they'll have to learn later will be taught to them by their German masters."[34]
>
> —Eric Koch, appointed Ukraine's commissar by Adolf Hitler.

Babi Yar

The Jewish population of Ukraine fared far worse during the Nazi occupation. The Nazis' special killing squads, the *Einsatzgruppen*, had killed thousands of Jews as the squads moved through Europe with the Nazi troops. However, their assignment in Kiev resulted in the highest number of deaths in the shortest amount of time; on September 29 and 30, 1941, the Nazis killed 33,771 Jews in Kiev.

The Jews of Kiev were told they were to be transferred to another location and were to bring their identification documents as well as warm clothing. However, they were taken just minutes away, herded into a ravine on the north edge of the city, known as Babi Yar, and shot. Between 1941 and 1943, about 70,000 more bodies—most of them Jews—were added to the mass grave. Historians estimate that as many as 120,000 people lie buried at the site—mostly Jews, but also some Ukrainian nationalists, gypsies, and others the Nazis deemed unnecessary.

After the war Soviet leaders refused to acknowledge Babi Yar with a war memorial. In fact, there were plans in the 1960s to build a housing project on the site of the ravine. However, thousands of Ukrainians protested. Soviet leaders ultimately allowed the site to be deemed a war memorial to Kiev's citizens who died there, but there was no mention that the vast majority of victims were Jews. Finally, after the dissolution of the Soviet Union in 1991, Ukraine's government allowed a menorah-shaped memorial to be erected on the site, finally honoring the memory of the tens of thousands of Jews buried there.

Religion Today

While all religions had been officially banned under communism, many people still risked severe punishment by worshipping in private. However, when Gorbachev became president, he relaxed the ban on religion somewhat. Though he did not condone Ukrainians and other Soviet people belonging to a church, he at least put an end to the intimidation and persecution of those who did practice a religion.

In 1991, after both the breakup of the Soviet Union and Ukraine's declaration of independence, millions of Ukrainians no longer had to be secretive about their faith. In addition to the growth of Catholicism and Orthodoxy, other Christian denominations, including Baptists, Lutherans, Mormons, and Methodists, have developed a presence in Ukraine. And, although many of Ukraine's Jews have left the country, in 2010 the Jewish population was estimated at sixty-seven thousand. In the Crimean Peninsula there are approximately 450,000 Muslims.

The Revival of Ukrainian Music

As the fall of the Soviet Union paved the way for people to worship openly, it also resulted in a great deal more hymns and other religious music being written and performed. For example, a religious opera called *Moses*, composed in 2001 by Myroslav Skoryk, was the first religiously themed opera written in Ukraine in one hundred years.

Although many of Ukraine's folk songs were lost with the *kobzari*, some of the folk traditions have enjoyed a revival, too—thanks to the efforts of brave individuals during Soviet times. While the Soviets were censoring and banning many of Ukraine's traditional folk songs because they were believed to promote religion or nationalism, some people were secretly documenting the songs. Since Ukraine became independent, some musicians began interviewing elderly Ukrainians who remembered melodies and words of many of the traditional songs, and have made recordings so future generations can listen to their musical heritage.

In the twenty-first century, a popular style of music among Ukrainian teens is Ukr-hop, Ukraine's version of American hip-hop music. One of the most famous bands is GreenJolly, whose song "Razom nas Bahato," ("We Are Many") became the unofficial anthem of Ukraine's Orange Revolution after the rigged election at first deprived Viktor Yushchenko of victory. The song reminds Ukrainians that they are determined not to be defeated and will not be fooled by government lies. "We Are Many" also reminds listeners that they are important in the struggle for freedom and that the time is drawing near for Ukraine to achieve that freedom. As a million protesters filled the *Maidan* in the days following the election, many—teens as well as adults—were inspired by GreenJolly's music.

Disagreements About Language

The most contentious social issue in post-Soviet Ukraine has been the status of spoken languages. In 1924 Stalin had decreed that Russian would be the official national language, completely banning the use of Ukrainian. But in 1995 the Russian language lost its status when Ukraine's legislature, the Rada, voted to make Ukrainian the national language.

However, in the years since then, those who live in the eastern and southern part of Ukraine demanded that Russian be elevated to the level of the official language in their part of Ukraine. Not surprisingly, the ethnic Ukrainians—most of whom live in the western part of the country—have held a deep-seated resentment against Russians since Ukraine was a Soviet republic. They insist that the Russian language should not be an official language anywhere in Ukraine.

The debate among legislators was fierce and confrontational. In one session of the Rada in March 2013, some legislators from eastern Ukraine began speaking in Russian, while the Ukrainian Liberty Party members drowned them out, yelling, "Speak Ukrainian!"[37] The verbal assaults soon became physical. In what was termed "The Rumble in the Rada" by some journalists, the lawmakers pulled hair, punched, and tried

Opposition lawmakers clash with deputies of the pro-presidential majority during a March 2013 session of Ukraine's parliament. A disagreement over the use of the Russian or Ukrainian language was one of the issues that led to the scuffle.

Return to Chernobyl

More than 116,000 people were evacuated from Chernobyl after the nuclear disaster in 1986. It was far too dangerous for people to remain, said experts. Most were resettled in housing projects hurriedly built on the outskirts of Kiev. In the years after the relocation, health professionals began noticing a sharp increase in anxiety and depression among the evacuees. They were lonely and missed their animals, their work, and their way of life.

As of 2014 about two hundred former Chernobyl residents had returned to the region known as the Exclusion Zone—the 18.6 mile (30 km) area around the reactor that is still considered highly dangerous. Residents in that area were evacuated by the USSR's military after the disaster. Most of the returnees are elderly widows. They have grown weary of living in the confines of the city—and the health risks have not deterred them.

Hanna Zavorotnya, whose cottage is located in what has been designated the Dead Zone of Chernobyl (a dangerous area), says government agents objected to anyone moving back—but she and her neighbors do not care. Now she has her chickens, her dog, and her pigs, and she loves being home despite the risks. "You can't take me from my mother; you can't take me from my motherland," she says. "Today I command the parade."

Quoted in *Telegraph* (UK), "The Women Living in Chernobyl's Toxic Wasteland," November 8, 2012. www.telegraph.co.uk.

to choke one another by pulling on neckties. One was even picked up by opposing party members and thrown over a banister as spectators in the gallery cheered.

The outcome was settled in August 2013, with the pro-Russian faction winning in a very close vote. President Viktor Yanukovych signed a bill giving Russian official language status in Russian-speaking parts of eastern and southern Ukraine. The opposition party was furious, and the threat that the legislation could cause an irreparable split in the country remains an ongoing worry for many Ukrainians.

CHAPTER FIVE

The Challenges Ahead

Throughout its history Ukraine has had to struggle with a wide range of difficult problems—from the effects of mass starvation and devastating wars to the worst nuclear accident in the planet's history. And while life in Ukraine has improved in some ways, there are still some formidable problems that the Ukrainian people must solve if they are to grow and thrive as a nation.

Chernobyl's Ghosts

Some of Ukraine's most challenging problems have to do with the health of its people. Since the Chernobyl explosion released ten tons of highly radioactive material into the atmosphere in 1986, medical experts have identified some disturbing health effects on the people of Ukraine and nearby areas—including Belarus, where 70 percent of the radioactive fallout settled.

According to a summary of a 2006 report by the European Committee on Radiation Risk, the occurrence of cancer in areas that received the nuclear fallout has increased 40 percent. The report also refers to studies showing a "wide range of chromosomal aberrations"[38] in the area surrounding Chernobyl. In other words, many of the children who survived may pass on deformities or other effects of the radiation to their own offspring.

The World Health Organization (WHO) also collected health data from the area and reported that thyroid cancer had increased one hundred times

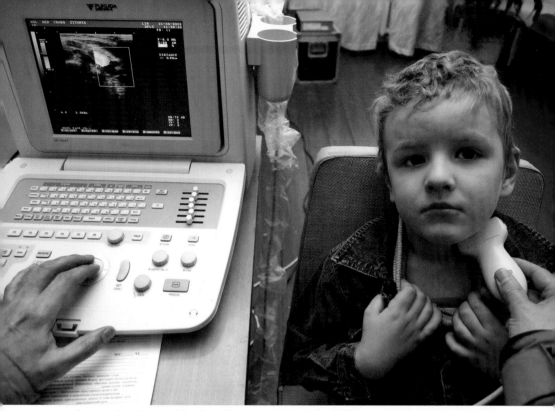

A young boy is tested for thyroid cancer at a mobile clinic in northwest Ukraine. Health experts say thyroid cancer, possibly caused by exposure to radiation released during the Chernobyl nuclear accident, is skyrocketing in children.

its normal rate. Especially worrisome to WHO was a skyrocketing increase in thyroid cancer in children—normally a disease not often seen in people under twenty-five. In fact, seven thousand children in Belarus, Russia, and Ukraine developed thyroid cancers between 1986 and 2005. In addition, in 2012 health experts announced that they had noticed a sharp increase in mouth cancers and birth defects in children born after Chernobyl's disaster.

Not surprisingly, the worst affected were those who received the most direct exposure, such as first responders. But many people who have become ill were eating produce grown on farms near Chernobyl for weeks before the government finally released information about the gravity of the nuclear accident—something that still angers many Ukrainian citizens.

Concerns About Polio

The effects of Chernobyl are by no means the only health issues in Ukraine. One of the most urgent health concerns is polio—a highly contagious crippling disease that has been virtually eradicated in the developed world. Though there is no cure yet for polio, the disease is easily prevented by immunizing babies under one year old. However, in November 2013 officials from WHO and the United Nations Children's Fund (UNICEF) warned of a threat of a recurrence of polio. Because most Ukrainian parents are not getting their children vaccinated, say health experts, a polio outbreak is a strong possibility there.

The risk is especially worrisome in Ukraine because cases of polio have appeared in Syria, where hundreds of Ukrainians are employed as engineers and construction workers. Israel, too, is a concern, because thousands of Israelis visit Ukraine each year. As of 2014 Israel has not had a full-blown case of polio, but doctors have found that several Israeli children carry the virus, which means that they can spread it to others.

And since Ukrainian children are not getting vaccinated, they are at special risk. Experts say that Ukraine's distrust of authority figures— in this case, physicians—may be to blame for the low vaccination rate. Many parents voice concerns that the vaccines may be tainted or of poor quality and could harm their children. Others worry that there could be dangerous side effects to the vaccine. As a result of these anxieties, parents ignore warnings from WHO and other medical authorities about the importance of polio vaccinations.

Health officials say that a 90 percent immunization rate is considered necessary to prevent polio outbreaks within a society. However, only between 30 and 50 percent of Ukrainian children have been immunized— and those numbers could be even lower. Many Ukrainian parents pay bribes to physicians to sign certificates of immunization, though their children have not received the immunizations.

Like many health professionals, Dorit Nitzan, Ukraine's representative to WHO, is convinced that an outbreak of polio is a foregone conclusion. "Recommending to people not to travel is no help," Nitzan says. "A virus does not know borders. We are really dealing [with] time now. It is no longer about 'if' but 'when.'"[39]

AIDS and Corruption

Another pressing health concern is the soaring rate of HIV and AIDS in Ukraine. In 2013 the number of HIV-infected Ukrainians was estimated as 450,000—approximately 1 percent of the nation's population. This marks a 20 percent increase since the year before. In October 2013 officials at WHO announced that within Central Asia and Eastern Europe, 90 percent of the new cases of HIV and AIDS are occurring in Ukraine and Russia. A great many of those infected are drug users who contracted the virus by sharing needles.

Health officials say that the problem of HIV and AIDS in Ukraine is far worse than it needs to be. There are powerful drugs on the market that can enable people to live fairly normal lives with the disease, but in a disturbing number of cases, they are not getting the drugs they need to survive. In fact, the AIDS death rate in Ukraine has gone up 20 percent because of lack of treatment.

Many believe that the blame can be placed squarely on the government—specifically Ukraine's Health Ministry. It is not that Ukraine lacks the money to purchase the AIDS drugs, say experts. They maintain that government employees have been purchasing life-extending AIDS drugs at highly inflated prices from middle-man companies, and in return, have been receiving kickbacks from those companies. And because the health officials spent so much on price-inflated drugs, they are not able to buy as much of the medicine as needed. As a result, only one in six AIDS patients have access to the much-needed drugs.

> "Corruption is a bulldozer that is destroying Ukraine."[40]
>
> —Hryhoriy, a retired police detective and AIDS patient, explaining why his medication is so hard to get.

One of these is Hryhoriy, a retired police officer who believes he contracted the disease when he donated blood years ago. Today he is furious that corruption is costing him and other vulnerable Ukrainians a chance at life. "If a patient is not receiving vital drugs, in the end he dies," he says. "Corruption is a bulldozer that is destroying Ukraine."[40]

A Nation of Bribes

The problem of corruption is pervasive in Ukraine, and it is not limited to the kickbacks associated with expensive HIV/AIDS medications.

In 2013, terminally ill Ukrainians, wearing cotton bags over their heads, protest the lack of government funds going toward treatment of diseases including HIV/AIDS and tuberculosis. Ukraine is experiencing a soaring rate of HIV/AIDS.

Ukraine has a far-reaching corruption problem and has consistently measured poorly on international corruption scales because of unfair elections, the acceptance of bribes by state officials, and the suppression of citizens' rights.

In fact, in a 2013 study called the Transparency International Corruption Perception Index, Ukraine ranks as the most corrupt country in Europe. And of the most corrupt 176 nations throughout the world (with 176 being the worst), Ukraine ranked 144th—tied with Iran, Nigeria, and the Central African Republic. Many diplomats—including those from the United States—have referred to Ukraine as a "kleptocracy," meaning a government that exists primarily to make its leaders wealthier.

Ukrainians see the evidence of corruption on a daily basis, says Liana, who emigrated with her family to the United States from Kiev in 1989. "Of course I've seen it. A day-to-day thing—it's so common everyone is used to it." She continues, "You get pulled over by a police officer, and he says, 'I pulled you over for speeding , and you say, 'No, no, I was driving at the speed limit like I was supposed to,' and he just looks at you and holds out his hand. Everyone knows what this is, it's happened to everybody in Ukraine. So you hand him $50 or maybe $100. The police, the government—everyone is taking bribes. That's Ukraine."[41]

William Smyth says the corruption is often heartbreaking, for it most often hurts those Ukrainians who cannot afford to pay expensive bribes.

> "The police, the government—everyone is taking bribes. That's Ukraine."[41]
>
> —Liana, a Ukrainian émigré, on the prevalence of corruption in Ukraine.

Smyth has a good friend in Ukraine whose boss called him into his office and told him that he had a debt that he could not pay: "My friend just looked at him and said, 'I don't have that much money! It's more than I make in six-month's time!' So the boss told him, 'Hey, if I pay this debt, I won't be able to afford to keep you on at your job. So my friend agrees to pay the debt in installments, just so he can keep the security of his job. We have been told repeatedly by Ukrainian friends that this kind of thing happens there very, very often."[42]

Dangers in the Workplace

In some cases economic corruption in Ukraine is resulting in physical danger to workers. One big concern of many people in coal-rich eastern Ukraine is the increasing number of illegal coal mines, known as *kopanki*. These mines are usually very small, often dug under buildings or even in the backyards of homes. Initially, many of these little mines were dug in the 1990s by families hoping to get a little extra coal for themselves for the winter.

In recent years, however, the *kopanki* have been acquired by investors who hired workers and bribed local authorities to look the other way. In 2013 the amount of coal mined in those small mines reached a new high—6 million tons, or about 10 percent of the total amount of coal mined in Ukraine. The *kopanki* have been extremely lucrative for the owners, who make millions of dollars each year. However, the profits do not reach the workers, either in wages, health insurance, or

Teenage Alcoholism in Ukraine

Amid the worries about the rising polio and AIDS rates in Ukraine, another health concern is alcoholism, especially among children. In 2008 the World Health Organization first published a report, "Ukrainian Teenagers Occupy First Place in the World in Alcohol Consumption." The following year UNICEF investigated and found that alcohol consumption among school age children has been increasing each year.

There are several aspects of this problem that experts say are disturbing. First, many children are having their first alcoholic drink between age ten and thirteen, and in 70 percent of cases, the drink is supplied by their parents. A second worry is the ease with which alcoholic beverages are bought in Ukraine. According to Ukraine Works, an organization working to reduce fetal alcohol syndrome in Ukraine, while the legal age to purchase alcohol is eighteen, many teens (and even younger children) go to kiosks, where vodka is sold on commission, and the salespeople rarely check IDs. Says twelve-year-old Michael, who purchased vodka at age ten, "I asked the sales assistant for a liter, pointed to the brand I wanted. She told me the price. I paid her and left. Ten minutes later, I returned for a second liter. The saleswoman said, 'You guys must be having quite a party.'"

Quoted in Michael Linden, "Buying Vodka Was So Easy," Ukraine Works LTD. www.ukraine worksltd.org.

even the most basic safety gear. Note reporters Ladka Bauerova and Kateryna Choursina, "Since they don't pay taxes, social security, or health insurance, or invest in safety equipment, the coal is five times cheaper [to produce] than what comes from the highly inefficient state mines."[43]

The miners they hire are just eager to have a job and are reluctant to voice any objections to the poor working conditions, even when their co-workers are hurt or killed in mining accidents. Because the mines tend to be shallow and are not dug by qualified engineers, sections occasionally collapse, killing workers and even causing damage to houses and streets in nearby residential areas.

East or West?

But while there are many issues that make life difficult for Ukrainians, none has been as volatile as the ongoing struggle to decide on a government that Ukrainians can agree on. Beginning in 2013 Ukraine's leaders were weighing the possibilities—whether the country should be joined politically and economically with Russia or with the European Union.

Ukraine's people are divided politically by region. Most of the eastern and southern industrial part of the country is made up primarily of ethnic Russians who are influenced in culture and trade by Russia. The majority of those favor an alliance with the Eurasian Economic Union, made up of Russia, Belarus, and Kazakhstan. On the other hand, those who live in the agricultural western section of Ukraine are far more interested in developing a partnership with Europe and the United States. In addition, many of Ukraine's younger generation—in both the east and the west—have embraced the values, culture, and politics of European countries.

In the fall of 2013 it seemed as though Ukraine president Viktor Yanukovich was leaning toward aligning Ukraine with the European Union (EU). But soon Vladimir Putin began putting pressure on Yanukovich, pushing him to join the Eurasian Economic Union. If Ukraine would not align with Russia, Putin warned, Russia would enact trade sanctions—something that would likely cripple Ukraine's already struggling economy.

Besides threatening punitive measures, Putin offered enticements. If Ukraine aligned with Russia, he guaranteed lower prices for natural gas that is so vital to Ukraine's economy. In addition, he offered a $15 billion stimulus package that would enable Ukraine to rebuild its crumbling infrastructure and pay off some of its international debts. Not surprisingly, Yanukovich suspended the process of integrating Ukraine with the EU.

Growing Fury

Furious that their president was planning to bow to Putin's demands, on December 8 hundreds of thousands of Ukrainians stormed into the *Maidan* where the Orange Revolution protests had taken place in 2004. There they protested, sang the Ukrainian national anthem, chanted antigovernment slogans, and toppled a statue of Lenin. Thousands of demonstrators shouted for the president and his advisers to resign. "Ukraine is tired of Yanukovich," one protester told reporters. "We need new rules, we need to completely change those in power. Europe can help us."[44]

In February 2014 Yanukovich announced that he had signed an accord to join the Russian-led Eurasian Economic Union—an action that further infuriated millions of Ukrainians. The beleaguered president fled Kiev on February 21, partly because of rising hostility toward his decision but also because of public outrage over allegations of corruption. Yanukovich was said to have used government funds to furnish his lavish country estate.

Takeover of Crimea

But a week later the world's attention shifted from the protests in Kiev to a spot 551 miles (887 km) away. The international community was astonished by the news that Vladimir Putin had mobilized Russian troops to invade Crimea, the peninsula on the Black Sea that was the southernmost part of Ukraine. Putin insisted that a referendum be held to allow the people of Crimea to decide whether they wished to secede from Ukraine.

Crimea's allure to Russia is its strategic location. As *Time* reporters David Von Drehle and Simon Shuster write, "Nations will seek to control Crimea as long as warriors and goods travel the world in ships."[45] Crimea is located at the mouth of Russia's Don River, and it is in a perfect spot to protect shipping routes between Russia, the southeastern part of Europe, and Turkey. It

> "Nations will seek to control Crimea as long as warriors and goods travel the world in ships."[45]
>
> —*Time* reporters David Von Drehle and Simon Shuster.

is also the home of Russia's Black Sea Fleet, which rents the space from Ukraine.

The United States, the European Union, and the interim government of Ukraine were outraged by Putin's referendum. Crimea had been an official part of Ukraine since Khrushchev gave it to Ukraine in 1954, when Ukraine was a Soviet Republic. But in the twenty-first century, Crimea's population is heavily Russian, and ethnic Ukrainians are in the minority. Given a choice in the referendum, 93 percent voted to secede, although some foreign journalists reported that pre-marked ballots (pro-secession) were being cast in Crimea.

Oleksandr Turchnyov, the acting president of Ukraine after Yanukovich's exit, calls the referendum "a farce, a fake, and a crime against the state."[46] The United States and its allies accused Russia of violating international law. Secretary of State John Kerry says, "You just don't in the 21st century behave in 19th century fashion by invading another country on completely trumped up pretext."[47]

Violence in Eastern Ukraine

The abrupt annexation of Crimea was followed by a worrisome spate of violence in eastern Ukraine. On April 10, 2014, satellite images revealed large numbers of Russian fighter jets, tanks, and other armored vehicles just thirty miles from the eastern border of Ukraine. In addition, approximately forty thousand Russian troops were deployed to the area. NATO military officials in Belgium who keep track of any unusual troop movements in Europe expressed concerned about the Russian buildup. "This is a capable force, ready to go," says Brigadier General Gary Deakin, who runs NATO's Belgium crisis operations center. "It has the resources to move quickly into Ukraine if it was ordered to do so. It is poised at the moment, and it could move very fast."[48]

On April 27 hundreds of armed pro-Russian separatists, many of them in what appeared to be Russian army uniforms but with insignias removed, took over a television station building in the large industrial

A resident of Ukraine's Donetsk region votes in a May 2014 referendum on the question of self-rule. The ballot measure, which passed, asked voters whether they supported self-determination but did not specifically mention independence or joining Russia.

city of Donetsk. An estimated five hundred Ukrainians gathered outside, demanding a referendum such as the one in Crimea, as they waved Russian flags and burned the yellow and blue flags of Ukraine. The scene was repeated in at least six other cities, where pro-Russian gunmen, aided by what appeared to be Russian troops, occupied government buildings, calling for secession from Ukraine.

In May 2014 residents of two regions of eastern Ukraine got their wish for a referendum. Although some residents boycotted the vote, a majority of those who took part in Donetsk and Luhansk voted in favor of self-rule. Some experts warned that the results were pushing Ukraine

The Presidential Palace

After President Viktor Yanukovych fled Kiev in February 2014, the lavish mansion he had built for himself was opened to the public and media. The massive estate is known as Mezhyhirya. Many wondered how a government official whose salary never exceeded $2,000 per month could afford to build and furnish such a luxurious five-story home on the banks of the Dnipro River. Valued at between $75 million and $100 million, the home sits on 340 acres (137 ha) of land and includes an indoor shooting range, a helipad, a golf course, a zoo, and an indoor swimming pool. Yanukovych reportedly has a fear of being poisoned, so he ordered greenhouses to be built on the premises so he could grow his own produce. That way he could be sure that his food was safe to eat.

The builder of the mansion, a German company called Honka, believes Mezhyhirya is the largest log-and-stone structure ever built. The company had even planned to nominate it for inclusion in the Guinness Book of World Records. The money spent on its furnishings may also set a record. Each door in the mansion is made from expensive Lebanese cedar costing $64,000, the copper trim and columns surrounding a single flight of steps cost nearly $430,000, and the overall price of imported furniture and carpeting was $9.4 million.

closer to civil war. The ballot measure did not specifically mention independence or joining Russia. Rather, it asked voters whether they supported self-determination, meaning the possibility of more autonomy but not necessarily breaking away from Ukraine. Regardless, the Ukraine government blasted the referenda and, as earlier, blamed incitement by Russian agents for the entire breakaway movement. Western powers, including the European Union and the United States, reacted negatively as well. They criticized the balloting as illegal and said they would not recognize the results of the votes.

By mid-2014 no one was certain whether eastern Ukraine would separate from western Ukraine or if some sort of reconciliation would be achieved. All that was certain was that very little has changed in Ukraine. It is still a land of great promise and bounty but also subject to the political whims of many competing forces.

SOURCE NOTES

Introduction: A Nation on the Brink

1. Quoted in Maria Danilova, "Prominent Ukrainian Activist and Journalist Brutally Beaten," *Business Insider*, December 25, 2013. www.businessinsider.com.
2. Quoted in *Kiev Ukraine News Blog*, "How Journalist Tetyana Chornovil Became the Face of Ukraine Struggle," December 26, 2013. http://news.kievukraine.info.
3. John Kerry, "Remarks with EU High Representative Catherine Ashton After Their Meeting," US Department of State, April 17, 2014. www.state.gov.

Chapter One: The Most Coveted Land

4. Anna Reid, *Borderland: A Journey Through the History of Ukraine.* Boulder, CO: Westview, 2000, p. 56.
5. Reid, *Borderland*, p. 30.
6. Quoted in Paul Kubicek, *The History of Ukraine.* Westport, CT: Greenwood, 2008, p. 39.
7. Reid, *Borderland*, p. 97.
8. Quoted in Kubicek, *The History of Ukraine*, p. 81.
9. Quoted in Peter J. Potichnyj et al., eds., *Ukraine and Russia in Their Historical Encounter.* Edmonton, AB: Canadian Institute of Ukraine Studies, 1992, p. 157.
10. Reid, *Borderland*, p. 100.
11. Thomas Prymak, *Mykhailo Hrushevsky.* Toronto: University of Toronto Press, 1995, p. 100.

Chapter Two: The Politics of Ukraine

12. Quoted in Reid, *Borderland*, p. 121.
13. Quoted in *Internet Modern History Sourcebook*, "Nikita S. Khrushchev: The Secret Speech—On the Cult of Personality, 1956," Fordham University. www.fordham.edu.

14. Yukechka, telephone interview by author, November 12, 2013.

15. Kubicek, *The History of Ukraine*, p. 114.

16. Kubicek, *The History of Ukraine*, p. 120.

17. Sergei Karastov, telephone interview by author, November 12, 2013.

18. Kubicek, *The History of Ukraine*, p 165.

19. Quoted in Paul Quinn-Judge and Yuri Zarakhovich, "The Orange Revolution," *Time*, November 28, 2004. http://content.time.com.

Chapter Three: The Economy of Ukraine

20. Quoted in Robert Conquest, *The Harvest of Sorrow: Soviet Collectivization and the Terror-Famine*. New York: Oxford University Press, 1986, p. 59.

21. Ryan Ver Berkmoes et al., *Russia, Ukraine, and Belarus*. Victoria, AU: Lonely Planet, 2000, p. 720.

22. Quoted in Daniel C. Diller, *Russia and the Independent States*. Washington, DC: *Congressional Quarterly*, 1993, p. 170.

23. Quoted in Tim Smith et al., *Ukraine's Forbidden History*. Stockport, UK: Dewi Lewis, 1998, p. 11.

24. Quoted in Smith et al., *Ukraine's Forbidden History*, p. 15.

25. Quoted in Library of Congress: Revelations from the Russian Archives, "Ukrainian Famine." www.loc.gov.

26. Kubicek, *The History of Ukraine*, p. 149.

27. Kubicek, *The History of Ukraine*, p. 149.

28. William Smyth, personal interview by author, January 25, 2014, Minneapolis, MN.

Chapter Four: The Social Fabric of Ukraine

29. Quoted in Reid, *Borderland*, p. 118.

30. Adriana Helbig et al., *Culture and Customs of Ukraine*. Westport, CT: Greenwood, 2009, p. 151.

31. Quoted in Conquest, *The Harvest of Sorrow*, p. 206.

32. Quoted in Samuel W. Mitcham Jr., *The German Defeat in the East, 1944–45*. Mechanicsburg, PA: Stackpole, 2001, p. 70.

33. Quoted in Smith et al., *Ukraine's Forbidden History*, p. 25.

34. Quoted in Mitcham Jr., *The German Defeat in the East*, p. 70.

35. Quoted in Laurence Rees, "A Warm Welcome Turns Cold in Nazi-Occupied Ukraine," HISTORYnet.com, November 5, 2012. www.historynet.com.

36. Quoted in Smith et al., *Ukraine's Forbidden History*, p. 26.

37. Quoted in RT, "Rada Riot: Ukrainian MPs Exchange 'Fascist' Insults, Start Brawl," March 19, 2013. http://rt.com.

Chapter Five: The Challenges Ahead

38. Quoted in Low Level Radiation Campaign (summary), "ECCR: Chernobyl 20 Years On. The Health Effects of the Chernobyl Accident." http://www.llrc.org/health/subtopic/ecrrchapteronesynopsis.htm#ref.

39. Quoted in *Huffington Post*, "Ukraine at Risk of Polio Outbreak Amid Low Vaccination Rate: WHO," November 15, 2013. www.huffingtonpost.com.

40. Quoted in Maria Danilova, "Ukraine: Corruption Blamed for AIDS Non-Treatment," Associated Press, June 29, 2012, http://bigstory.ap.org.

41. Liana, personal interview by author, January 13, 2014, St. Louis Park, MN.

42. Smyth, personal interview by author.

43. Ladka Bauerova and Kateryna Choursina, "Ukraine's Illegal Coal Mines Lure Desperate Workers," *Bloomberg Businessweek*, November 17, 2013. www.businessweek.com.

44. Quoted in CBS News, "Ukrainian Protesters Topple Lenin Statue in Kiev," December 8, 2013. www.cbsnews.com.

45. David Von Drehle and Simon Schuster, "What Putin Wants," *Time*, March 6, 2014, pp. 24–25.

46. Quoted in *Guardian* (UK), "Ukrainian Crisis: Crimean MPs' Vote to Join Russian Federation Sparks Outrage," March 6, 2014. www.theguardian.com.

47. Quoted in Will Dunham, "Kerry Condemns Russia's 'Incredible Act of Aggression' in Ukraine," Reuters, March 2, 2014. www.reuters.com.

48. Quoted in *Guardian* (UK), "Satellite Images Reveal Russian Military Buildup on Ukraine's Border," April 10, 2014. www.theguardian.com.

FACTS ABOUT UKRAINE

Geography

- Location: Eastern Europe.
- Area: 233,032 sq. miles (603,550 sq. km), slightly smaller than Texas.
- Coastline: 1,728.65 miles (2,782 km).

People and Society

- Population: 44,573,205 (as of July 2013).
- Median age: 40.3 years.
- Population living in cities: 69.9 percent.
- Ethnicity: 77.8 percent Ukrainian; 17.3 percent Russian; 4.9% other ethnicities.
- People living with HIV/AIDS: 230,500 (as of 2012).

Government

- Type of government: republic.
- Capital: Kyiv (sometimes spelled Kiev).
- Provinces (similar to states): twenty-four.
- Voting age: eighteen years and older.
- Frequency of presidential elections: every five years.

Economy

- National GDP (purchasing power): $331.6 billion (2012).
- Average per capita GDP: $7,300.
- Top agricultural products: grain, sugar beets, sunflower seeds, vegetables, beef, milk.
- Top industrial products: coal, electric power, metals, machinery.
- Unemployment rate: 7.5 percent.
- Population living below the poverty line: 24.1 percent.

Transportation

- Airports (paved and unpaved runways): 187.
- Railways: 13,433 miles (21,619 km).
- Roads (paved and unpaved): 105,443 miles (169,694 km).
- Major seaports: Feodosiya, Illichivsk, Mariupol, Mykolayiv, Odessa, Yuzhnyy.

FOR FURTHER RESEARCH

Books

Daniel Barter, *Chernobyl's Atomic Legacy: 25 Years After Disaster*. Tours, France: Jonglez, 2012.

Volodymyr Bassis and Sakina Dhilawala, *Ukraine*. New York: Marshall Cavendish, 2009.

Marc Di Duca, Leonid Ragozin, and Sarah Johnstone, *Ukraine*. London: Lonely Planet, 2011.

Adriana Helbig, Oksana Buranbaeva, and Vanja Mladineo, *Culture and Customs of Ukraine*. Westport, CT: Greenwood, 2012.

Will Mara, *The Chernobyl Disaster*. New York: Marshall Cavendish, 2011.

Anna K. Shevchenko, *Culture Smart! Ukraine*. London: Kuperard, 2012.

Websites

Guide to Ukraine (http://ukraine.uazone.net). This English-language site has maps, articles on Ukraine's history and culture, as well as news articles about events occurring throughout the country.

InfoUkes (www.infoukes.com/religion). This site provides information about religion, politics, and travel in Ukraine, as well as political satire.

KyivPost (www.kyivpost.com). *KyivPost* is the online weekly edition of Ukraine's largest English-language newspaper. It features in-depth articles about politics and economic and social issues.

The World Factbook (https://www.cia.gov/library/publications/the-world-factbook/geos/up.html). The World Factbook is a website of the US Central Intelligence Agency. It contains detailed statistics on the geography, economy, transportation, government, history, and people of Ukraine.